STEPHEN LIFF

Landmark
BOOKS

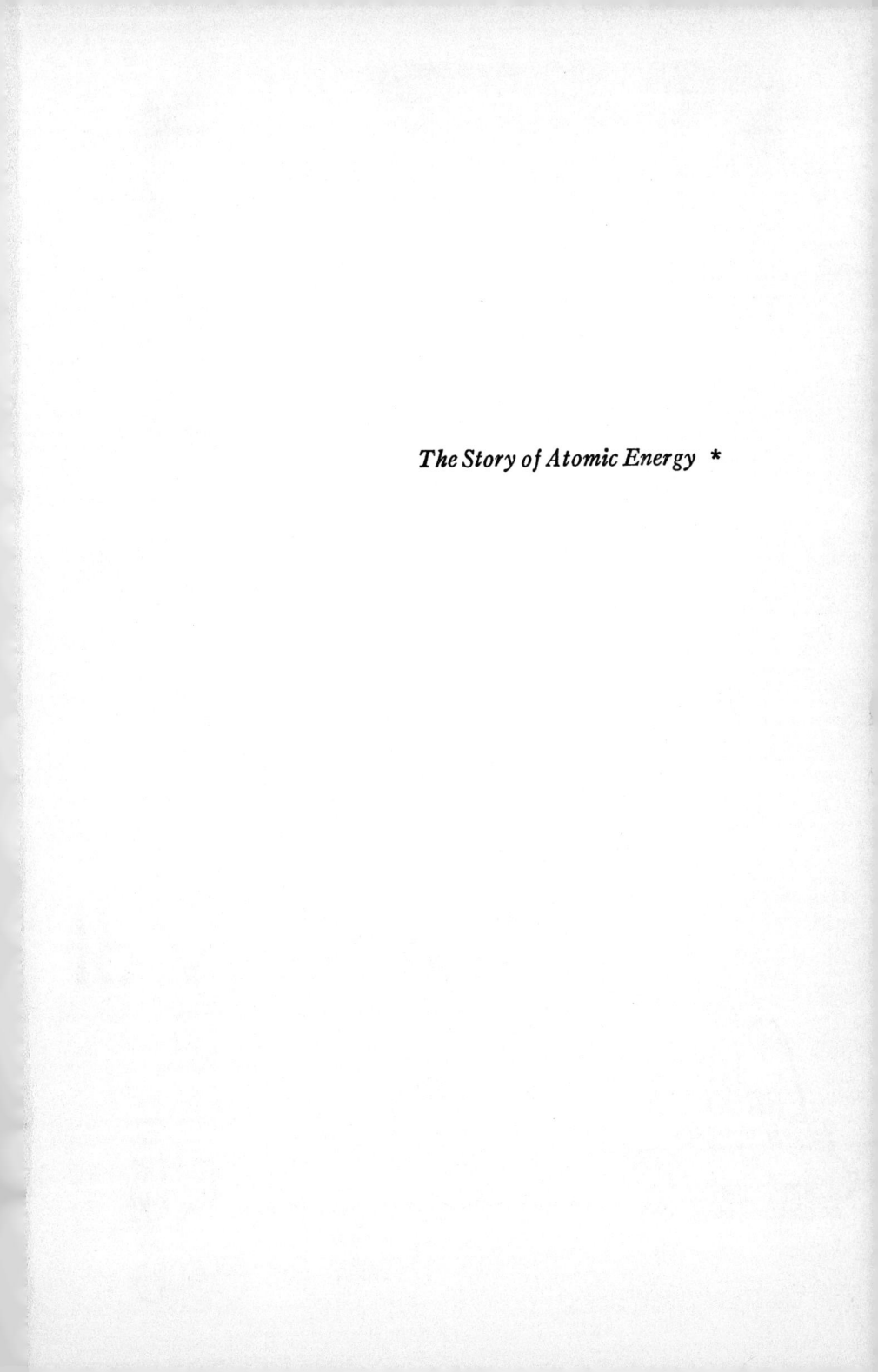

The Story of Atomic Energy *

The Story of

Landmark
BOOKS

Random House New York

ATOMIC ENERGY
by Laura Fermi

Acknowledgments

In the preparation of this book I was assisted by several persons who gave me the benefit of their experience, source material or photographs. To all I wish to express my deep appreciation.

I owe special thanks to Professor Eugene P. Wigner of Princeton University for his friendly criticism; to Professor Samuel K. Allison of the University of Chicago, Doctor John Marshall of the Los Alamos National Laboratory and Professor Emilio Segré of the University of California for their personal recollections; to Professor Otto Hahn of Goettingen, Germany, for letting me draw on his articles on fission; and to Professor Arthur Holly Compton and Oxford University Press for permission to reprint two anecdotes from his *Atomic Quest*.

LAURA FERMI

First Printing

© Copyright, 1961, by Laura Fermi
All rights reserved under International and Pan-American Copyright Conventions. Published in New York by Random House, Inc., and simultaneously in Toronto, Canada, by Random House of Canada, Limited.
Library of Congress Catalog Card Number: 61-7589
Manufactured in the United States of America, by H. Wolff

To my friend Clifton Anderson
who took time from his fifth
grade work to read the manuscript
of this book and discuss it with me.

Contents

1. Atom means indivisible, but . . . * 3 *
2. . . . Atoms are not indivisible * 10 *
3. A new kind of artillery * 25 *
4. Better bullets * 34 *
5. The riddle of element 93 * 45 *
6. Uranium and the Second World War * 61 *
7. Birth of the atomic age * 73 *
8. Plans for three secret cities * 90 *
9. The city that made uranium 235 * 101 *
10. The city that made plutonium * 108 *
11. The most secret of the secret cities * 118 *
12. Atoms for peace * 132 *
13. Power from the atoms * 142 *
14. Radioisotopes for better living * 155 *

Index * 179 *

The Story of Atomic Energy *

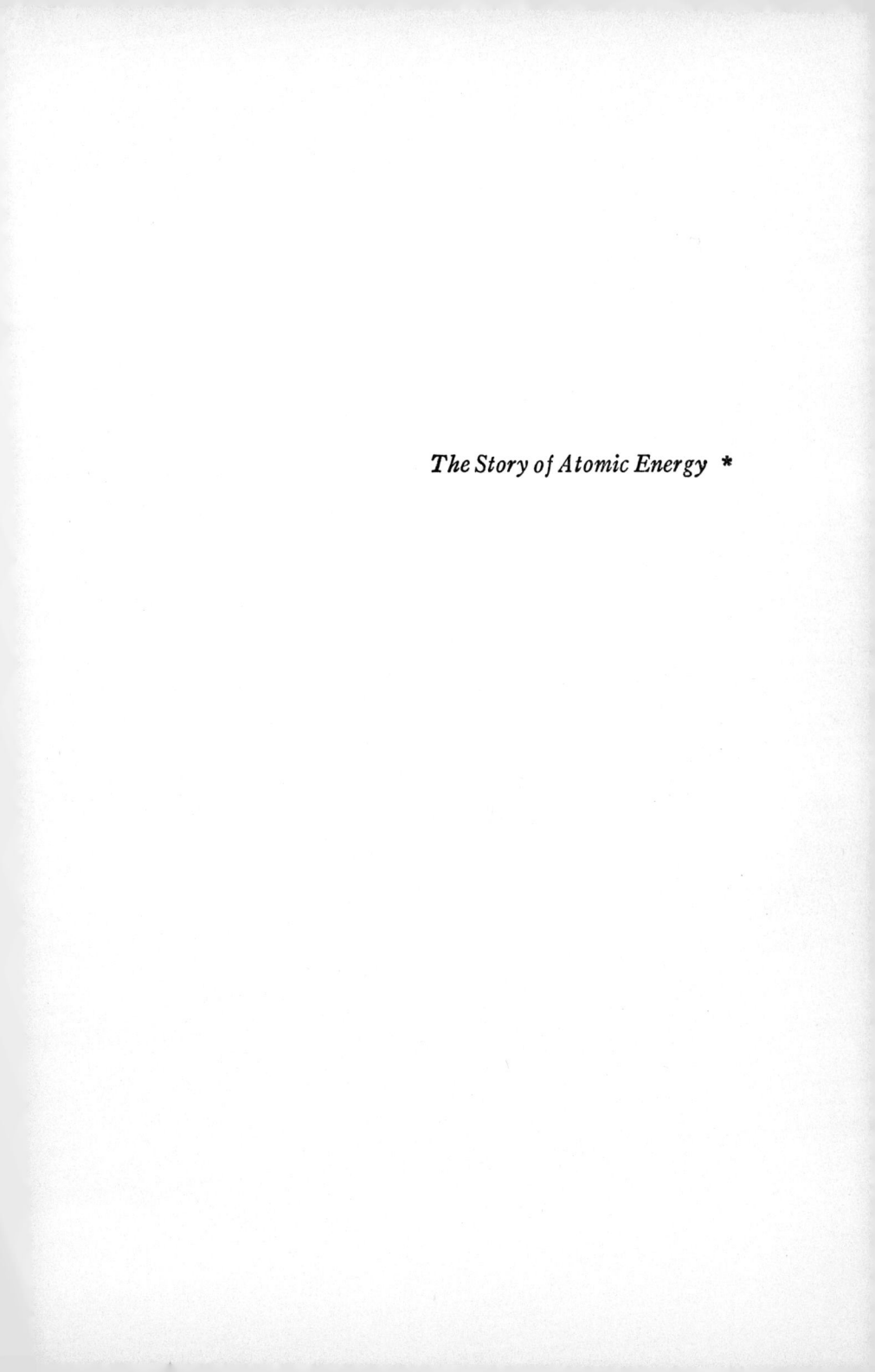

1

Atom means indivisible, but...

This is a story of discovery and invention. It will take us through many centuries, and to many countries in which men and women have studied the nature of atoms. It will show us these men and women at work, learning slowly, step by step, how atoms are made and what they can do. Our story will permit us to view the modern world of atomic energy, and will give us glimpses of the world of future times.

Today we know that atoms are the tiny particles of

The Story of Atomic Energy

which all matter is made. But who was the first person to think about atoms? We cannot answer this question; ideas form slowly and are based on older ideas. As long as there have been thinking men on our earth they have asked themselves many questions about the world around them. Many must have thought, "We see a great variety of things in nature—the sun, moon, and stars, mountains and seas, forests and animals. We can make objects, too. All these things look different. Is it possible that they are made of a few simpler elements?" To this question, we cannot know how many men have answered: "Perhaps everything is made of small particles."

Long, long ago, some philosophers took up this idea. One of them was Democritus, who lived in ancient Greece some 2400 years ago. We know about Democritus and his thought, because some of his writings have come down to us. But there may have been many others who had similar ideas. Democritus said that everything was made of tiny particles, or corpuscles, so small that no one could see them. They grouped to-

Atom means indivisible, but . . .

gether in different ways to form the different substances. The particles themselves could never change, and they could not be broken down into smaller particles. Democritus called them atoms, from the Greek word *atomos*, which means "indivisible." According to him, atoms were the smallest particles that could exist.

Democritus's thought ran somewhat along these lines: Let us look at a substance like water. We may take a very small amount of it, a single drop, and with some care we may divide this drop into two tiny droplets. If it were possible to get the proper tools and equipment, we might be able to go on making tinier and tinier droplets. But could we go on forever? The philosophers who thought as Democritus did believed that at a certain point we would obtain a droplet that could not be cut into smaller parts. The smallest pieces into which water (or any other substance) could be cut were the atoms.

Because Democritus did not base his views on facts, he could not prove them. For centuries, very few persons believed that atoms really existed. More people thought that atoms were the fruit of Democritus's imagination. But in the last 350 years, as modern science developed, physicists and chemists gradually went back to Democritus's ideas.

In the early seventeenth century, for instance, the great Italian scientist Galileo said that perhaps he could explain odors and tastes by supposing that some substances dissolve into small corpuscles. These corpuscles might hit sensitive spots in our tongues and nostrils, and create the familiar sensations. It later developed that Galileo was right.

Toward the end of the same century, the English chemist Robert Boyle said that air and all other gases behaved as if they were made of corpuscles. More and more facts were being explained by admitting that atoms existed.

2

It was an Englishman, John Dalton, who first expressed a scientific *atomic theory*. Dalton was born in

Atom means indivisible, but . . .

1766, the son of a poor weaver in a village in Cumberland. As a child John went to the village school, which was small and had only one teacher. When John was twelve, the teacher retired, and John took his place. From then on young Dalton supported himself by teaching. He was greatly interested in science, and while he taught he studied mathematics and chemistry by himself. At the age of twenty-seven he became a college instructor.

In the century before Dalton's birth, chemists had come to recognize an important fact: while they could separate some substances into simpler substances, there were others they could never separate. For example, chemists could separate water into hydrogen and oxygen, table salt into chlorine and sodium, sugar into carbon and water. But they could never obtain simpler substances from hydrogen, oxygen, carbon, chlorine, and sodium. These simple substances were given the name *chemical elements*. Such substances as water, salt, and sugar, which are made of more than one element, were called *chemical compounds*. We

The Story of Atomic Energy

now know that there are over one hundred elements, but in Dalton's time only some thirty elements were known.

Dalton asked himself whether atoms might help explain the existence of elements and the differences in their properties. After much thinking and many experiments he reached some fundamental conclusions, which he published around 1810.

Dalton's theory is important. It shows that an atom of a given element, small as it is, has all the features of that element. If we could enlarge an atom, for instance an iron atom, and look at it, we would be able to tell that it was iron. We would not mistake it for hydrogen, sodium, or any other element. It would not matter which iron atom we enlarged, for, as Dalton said, all iron atoms are alike. (Likewise, all sodium atoms are alike, all hydrogen atoms are alike, and so on.)

Dalton also explained that atoms of different chemical elements may combine to form chemical compounds. For example, two hydrogen atoms may com-

Atom means indivisible, but . . .

bine with one oxygen atom and form a *molecule* of water. One chlorine atom may combine with one sodium atom and form a molecule of salt.

This is, in short, Dalton's atomic theory. It has explained many facts, and from it modern chemistry has grown. Yet, although Dalton's theory was correct on the whole, one of his views had to be discarded. Like Democritus, John Dalton said that atoms are the smallest particles into which matter divides—that atoms are indivisible. Most scientists shared this view until fifty years after his death. Then the work of several physicists proved that atoms can break down into smaller pieces. This work began in France with an important discovery, and now we are going to see how this discovery took place.

2

... Atoms are not indivisible

1

In early 1896, in Paris, the French physicist Henri Becquerel was testing a number of phosphorescent substances. These are substances that glow for a while after they have been exposed to sunlight or other radiation. They are described as "phosphorescent" or "phosphorus-like" because they act like the element phosphorus, which also glows if it has been in the light.

Becquerel found by accident that when a phosphorescent uranium salt is glowing, it gives off not only

. . . Atoms are not indivisible

light but also another radiation. He had wrapped a photographic plate in thick black paper through which light could not go. Then he had placed a small piece of uranium salt on the wrapped plate and exposed it to sunlight. When he developed the plate he found that the piece of uranium salt had made its silhouette in black on the plate. The radiation that it had given off had gone through the black paper. As physicists say, it was more *penetrating* than light—it could go through materials that stopped light.

A few days later he discovered something even stranger: the uranium salt could give off the more penetrating radiation even if he had not exposed it to sunlight, but had kept it a long time in a dark place. In other words, it gave off the radiation *spontaneously*!

This is what happened: Becquerel, not satisfied with the result of a single experiment, wished to test the glow of the uranium salt once more. To do this, he had taken several plates, each wrapped in thick black paper; over each plate he placed a small piece of uranium salt. He would have then exposed the

The Story of Atomic Energy

plates to sunlight, but meanwhile the weather had changed. The sky was covered with clouds and there was no sunshine. Becquerel put his plates away in a drawer, each with its piece of uranium salt on top. He waited for a few days, but still the weather did not clear up, and he developed the plates, expecting to find faint images on them. To his surprise, he found, instead, strong silhouettes of the pieces of uranium salt. While it had been in the drawer the uranium salt had given off the penetrating radiation.

Becquerel's curiosity was aroused and he tested many other substances containing uranium. All gave off radiation spontaneously. From this he concluded that uranium was the element that gave off radiation —but was it the only one that behaved this way? He had found no other.

. . . Atoms are not indivisible

2

Sometime later a young married woman, Madame Marie Curie, did discover other elements that behaved like uranium.

Marie was born in Poland and had worked there as a children's governess until she had put aside enough money to study in France. As a student in the University of Paris, she had worked very hard until she had obtained a degree in physics and one in mathematics.

Marie was pretty, with fine blonde ringlets around a soft, intelligent face. She had never seemed to be aware of her looks, for she had been too absorbed in her work. Then she had met Pierre Curie, a professor of physics as devoted to science as she was. Pierre Curie had noticed both her looks and her intelligence. They married, and in the fall of 1897 a baby daughter, Irene, was born to them. (Later they had a second daughter, Eve.)

The Story of Atomic Energy

Shortly after Irene's birth, Madame Curie decided to take up the study of the rays that Becquerel had discovered almost two years before. Pierre approved the choice and provided the few instruments needed for her research. Patiently she began to test all known elements, one after the other. At last she was rewarded. The element *thorium*, like uranium, gave off a radiation spontaneously. Here was proof that this activity was not a property of uranium alone. Marie and Pierre Curie called the property *radioactivity*, which is short for radiating activity.

3

To learn more about radioactivity, Madame Curie went on testing materials. One day as she worked with a piece of a uranium ore called pitchblende, she was astonished to find that it gave off a radiation much stronger than the radiation from uranium and thorium.

. . . Atoms are not indivisible

She measured the intensity of the radiation over and over again, to make sure that she had not made a mistake, but the result was always the same. She concluded that the piece of pitchblende must contain a new and unknown radioactive element. The amount of this element in the pitchblende was so small that Madame Curie could not see it. Only the strong radiation revealed its presence.

Marie and Pierre Curie were excited by this problem. Pierre gave up his own work, and together they began to look for the new radioactive element in the pitchblende. After months of patient research they discovered an element that Marie called *polonium,* after Poland, the country of her birth. Six months later they found that pitchblende contained another element which gave off an even stronger radiation than polonium. They called this element *radium.*

When the Curies tried to isolate pure radium from the pitchblende, they faced great difficulties. There was so little radium in the pitchblende that they would

The Story of Atomic Energy

have to treat hundreds and hundreds of pounds before they could obtain from it even a tiny sample of pure radium.

To do this, the Curies needed a larger place than the little room where they had been working. The only space they could find was an old woodshed in the courtyard of the School of Physics where Pierre was teaching. The shed was cold and damp. It had no floor, and on rainy days the roof leaked. It was far from an ideal laboratory. Yet in that shed Marie Curie spent the happiest years of her life, sharing her work with her husband.

At the end of four years of research the Curies had treated several tons of pitchblende and had obtained one-tenth of a gram of a pure radium salt. One-tenth of a gram is a very small amount, little more than a speck; it takes twenty-eight grams to make one ounce. Yet, using this fragment, Marie could study the properties of radium. Its activity, she found, was over one million times greater than the activity of an equal weight of uranium.

. . . Atoms are not indivisible

Radium proved to be extremely useful, both in research—for the study of the nature of atoms—and in medicine—for the treatment of cancer.

The study of radium and radioactivity became Marie's life work. She kept it up after her husband was run over by a horse-drawn cart and killed in 1906. Madame Curie carried on alone the work that they had started together, and she was able to make other great contributions to science.

Shortly after the Curies had discovered polonium and radium, other scientists found a few more radioactive substances. It became clear that radioactivity was much more widespread in nature than scientists had thought.

4

The discovery of radioactivity raised many questions. Scientists wondered about the radiation given off by uranium and other radioactive materials. What was it

The Story of Atomic Energy

made of? Where did it come from? How was it produced? Did any change take place in the materials that gave off radiation? The physicist who did most to answer these questions was Ernest Rutherford.

Rutherford was born on a farm in New Zealand and had gone to college in that country. There is a story that he was digging potatoes when he received the news that he had won a scholarship to study physics in Cambridge, England. This was a great piece of luck for young Ernest, because in England he was to work with one of the most famous physicists of his time, J. J. Thomson.

Rutherford left for England a few months before Becquerel discovered the strange radiation from uranium. While Rutherford was in Cambridge, J. J. Thomson discovered the existence of very tiny particles charged with negative electricity; he called them *electrons*. Thomson measured the charge and mass of electrons, and Rutherford helped him with some of this work. The measurements showed that all electrons are alike, that each electron carries one negative

* 18 *

. . . Atoms are not indivisible

charge and is about 1800 times lighter than the lightest atom, hydrogen.

The news of the discovery of radioactivity reached Rutherford while he was helping Thomson. At once his alert mind felt the challenge of the problems raised by radioactivity. He would have liked to start working immediately in the new field, but this was not possible. He had been appointed professor of physics at the University of Montreal in Canada and he had first to move there. He was then barely twenty-seven years old.

Rutherford arrived in Montreal at about the time when Marie and Pierre Curie were settling in the old shed to begin to separate radium from pitchblende. The young professor had much better luck than the Curies, for in Montreal he headed one of the best physics laboratories in existence at that time; it had been paid for by a tobacco millionaire. There Rutherford had several young people to help him, and money to spend for his research. As soon as he settled down, he began working on radioactivity.

But scientific research is slow and painstaking. Even in the excellent conditions of his new laboratory it took Rutherford a few years to understand fully the nature of the radiation from uranium and other radioactive elements. He found that this radiation is made of several kinds of rays. One is a stream of very fast particles charged with positive electricity. He called these rays *alpha rays,* and the particles *alpha particles.* Later he ascertained that an alpha particle is about four times as heavy as a hydrogen atom, and that it carries two positive charges.

A second kind of rays, he found, is a stream of very fast particles charged with negative electricity. Rutherford called these *beta rays,* and the particles of which they are made *beta particles.* It did not take him long to recognize that beta particles are very fast electrons —he knew electrons well from his work with Thomson.

A French physicist found a third kind of rays, *gamma rays.* They are similar to light rays and x-rays, but more penetrating.

. . . Atoms are not indivisible

Scientists agreed that alpha, beta, and gamma rays must come from atoms; they could not come from anything else. Then, if atoms could give off fast particles and gamma rays, two new revolutionary concepts emerged. First, it was not true that atoms are indivisible, as Democritus, Dalton, and many others had thought. Second, atoms must contain large amounts of energy.

Rutherford gave an explanation of radioactive changes. He suggested that atoms of radioactive elements can break down and that some of them do. He also suggested that when a radioactive atom breaks down, it gives off either an alpha particle or a beta particle, and often also gamma rays. Rutherford said that when radioactive atoms break down, *they change into different atoms.*

This statement was astonishing. For centuries men had tried to change one element into another by chemical means, but they had never had any success. Finally they had come to the conclusion that it was im-

The Story of Atomic Energy

possible to change one element into another. Now Rutherford suggested that some elements could change spontaneously into other elements.

Rutherford was right. He and other scientists proved that radioactive elements do change. When a radium atom breaks down, for instance, it gives off an alpha particle and gamma rays, and it changes into the atom of an element called radon. There is no doubt that radium and radon are different elements; radium is a solid metallic substance, radon is a gas. Like radium, radon is radioactive and gives off alpha particles.

The radioactive change of one element into another is often called "decay" by physicists. They say, for instance, that radium decays into radon.

Rutherford found that, as a piece of radioactive substance decays, its activity decreases. If at first a piece of substance was giving off, let's say, one thousand particles per second, it might, after a while, give off only nine hundred particles per second. After a longer time it would give off an even smaller number of particles. There would be a time after which the piece

. . . Atoms are not indivisible

of substance would give off only 500 particles per second, half as many particles as it was giving off at first. Its activity would be only one half what it was at first.

Rutherford gave the name *half life* to the time in which the activity of a piece of a radioactive substance is cut down to one half. This period of time is different for each radioactive substance. Some substances decay very slowly; their activity also decreases very slowly, and their half life is very long. The half life of uranium is 4500 millions of years. The half life of radium is 1560 years. Other substances decay much faster, and their half life may be a fraction of a second.

These were exciting findings. Just as exciting was the thought that a tiny particle like the atom must contain enormous amounts of energy. Atoms break down with explosive violence, and pieces of atoms, alpha and beta particles, fly off at tremendous speeds— beta particles may fly off at half the speed of light or even faster. This means that alpha and beta particles have very great energy. Additional energy comes out of atoms in the form of gamma rays. Energy is never created. If atoms can give off energy, they must contain it.

Scientists began to talk of the immense "store of energy" locked up in the atoms and of the enormous amount of work that this energy could do if men were to learn to get it out of atoms and control its flow. To most scientists of that time, this seemed to be idle talk, a wild dream that would never come true.

3

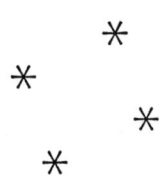

A new kind of artillery

1

The study of radioactive changes helped scientists to understand the nature of atoms; in turn, learning about atoms helped them to clarify their ideas about radioactivity. Slowly the pieces of the picture fell into place.

In 1919, before the picture was complete, Rutherford had a brilliant idea that sped up the pace of discovery. (He was then back in England, where he was

The Story of Atomic Energy

to stay for the rest of his life.) His idea was to use alpha particles as "bullets" to bombard atoms.

In the small world of the atom, alpha particles are nice big chunks. They come out of radioactive substances with great speed and energy. Rutherford thought that if he used them as bullets, he might be able to smash atoms. If he succeeded, the pieces into which the atoms broke might help him to learn how atoms are made.

His powerful "gun" was a small gram of radium, which shot alpha particles with enormous force. With it Rutherford kept some nitrogen under heavy bombardment. Some of the alpha particles hit nitrogen atoms right in their centers, broke them down, and made chips fly off. When Rutherford examined these chips he found that they were particles never observed before. They had the same mass as hydrogen atoms and carried one positive charge each. Later they were called *protons*.

After Rutherford's success, many other physicists used this same kind of artillery to shoot at atoms.

A new kind of artillery

Bombardment of atoms proved a very useful method of research.

In 1932 the English physicist James Chadwick bombarded beryllium—a light metal—with alpha particles. He found that under alpha bombardment beryllium gave off particles with the same mass as hydrogen and no electric charge. These particles had already been given a name: they were called *neutrons*. For a long time physicists had guessed that neutrons existed and had talked about them, but had been unable to find them.

2

The neutron was the last piece in the picture of the atom. Many years before, Rutherford had suggested the outline of the picture. An atom, he had said, must be made of a tiny nucleus charged with positive electricity, and of electrons moving around the nucleus. Rutherford's friend, the Danish physicist Niels Bohr, had worked out a mathematical explanation that showed how the electrons move around the nucleus. (Bohr was to become one of the most famous of the world's atomic physicists.)

As Rutherford and Bohr had suggested, an atom is made of a tiny nucleus and of electrons moving around it. The nucleus is made of protons and neutrons. The number of protons, electrons, and neutrons is different for different elements. There is, however, a general plan for all elements. In each atom the number of protons in the nucleus is equal to the number of electrons that circle around it. Since each proton carries one positive charge and each electron one negative charge, the atom is neutral. In any one element, all the nuclei have the same number of protons. This number is called the *atomic number*.

Electrons have practically no mass. Protons and neutrons account for the entire mass of an atom. A proton is said to have mass 1. A neutron also has mass 1.

The simplest atom is hydrogen. It is made of a sin-

A new kind of artillery

gle proton around which moves a single electron. The atomic number of hydrogen is 1, and its *atomic mass* is also 1.

Helium is the next element. Its nucleus is made of two protons and two neutrons. Two electrons circle around it. Its atomic number is 2 and its mass is 4. The mass of helium is four times the mass of hydrogen.

The most complex atom found on the earth is uranium. All uranium atoms are made of 92 electrons circling about a nucleus in which there are 92 protons. There are, however, three slightly different varieties of uranium, each with a slightly different number of neutrons in their nuclei. The nuclei of the most common variety contain 146 neutrons in addition to the 92 protons. The atomic mass of this variety is then $92 + 146$, or 238. The nuclei of the other two varieties contain 143 and 142 neutrons respectively. The atomic masses of these varieties are then 235 and 234.

Other elements also come in varieties whose nuclei contain slightly different numbers of neutrons. These varieties of elements are called *isotopes*. We may then say that there are three isotopes of uranium. They are uranium 238, uranium 235, and uranium 234.

3

Although the discovery of neutrons completed the picture of the atom, physicists went on bombarding atoms. Atomic bombardments had opened new possibilities, new leads that were worth following. Not only had they revealed the particles of which nuclei are made, they had also proved that some elements which are not radioactive and do not change spontaneously can be changed into other elements.

When Rutherford had bombarded nitrogen with alpha particles (and discovered the protons), each nitrogen atom that had been hit had captured an alpha particle and had given off a proton. These nitrogen atoms had changed into oxygen atoms. When Chadwick had bombarded beryllium (and discovered the

A new kind of artillery

neutrons), each beryllium atom that had been hit had captured an alpha particle and given off a neutron. These beryllium atoms had changed into carbon atoms. Other scientists had bombarded a few other light elements and produced similar changes.

To be sure, the amounts of elements changed were extremely small. No one could see them or weigh them. Yet the scientists expected that if they went on breaking atoms they would learn more secrets about matter, and discover more laws of nature.

Among the scientists who had become skilled in handling atomic artillery was Madame Curie's daughter Irene. She had been born, as was stated earlier, shortly before her mother started the study of the radiation from uranium. She had grown into a serious child who liked to study and learn, then into a young woman with her parents' love for science. Like her mother, she became a physicist and married a physicist, Frédéric Joliot.

Irene and Frédéric began to work together as Madame Curie's assistants and learned from her to work with radioactive substances. Later they undertook the bombardment of atoms.

In 1933 they were bombarding aluminum with alpha particles when they noticed something they had not foreseen. As the hit aluminum atoms broke down, they changed into atoms that gave off a radiation and behaved like radioactive atoms. The Joliots found that the bombarded aluminum had changed into a radioactive isotope of phosphorus that does not exist in nature. Years before, Becquerel and Madame Curie had discovered *natural radioactivity,* radioactivity that occurs spontaneously in nature. Now Irene and Frédéric Joliot had discovered artificial—man-made—*radioactivity.*

This was an important discovery. Madame Curie was very much pleased, and quite proud of Irene and Frédéric, the more so because she could no longer do active research herself. She was old and ill with an incurable form of anemia. This was probably caused by the radiation of the substances she had handled; in the

A new kind of artillery

early days following the discovery of radioactivity, scientists had not known that radiations were dangerous and they had not taken the precautions observed today. Madame Curie died a few months after the Joliots' discovery of artificial radioactivity. Her younger daughter, Eve, wrote a moving book about her life which reveals Madame Curie's deep love for science and describes her great achievements.

4

Better bullets

1

The discovery of artificial radioactivity stirred up a great interest among physicists—and not only in France. As soon as the news reached Italy, the young physicist Enrico Fermi decided that he too would try to produce artificial radioactivity. He thought that if he used neutrons for bullets, instead of alpha particles, he might be able to produce radioactivity not only in light elements, but in heavier ones, too.

The reason is simple. Alpha particles are positively

Better bullets

charged and when they go through matter they are affected in two ways: on the one hand, the negatively charged electrons circling around nuclei attract alpha particles and slow them so rapidly that soon these stop altogether. Alphas travel a short path and their chances of finding a nucleus on it are small. On the other hand, if an alpha particle does manage to come in contact with a nucleus, it is repelled by the positive charge of the protons in the nucleus; the alpha loses energy and may not hit the nucleus hard enough to break it. But neutrons have no electric charge; they are neither attracted by electrons nor repelled by nuclei; their path is much longer than that of alpha particles and their speed and energy are greater; so Fermi thought that they would have a better chance of hitting nuclei and smashing them.

Neutrons, however, do not come out of radioactive substances spontaneously, as do alpha particles. Men must make neutrons by bombarding an element like beryllium with alpha particles, and it takes almost 100,000 alpha particles to produce one neutron.

The Story of Atomic Energy

By using neutrons, instead of alpha particles, Fermi was going to have better bullets, but fewer of them. For this reason he could not tell in advance whether bombardment with neutrons would be successful. He had to try.

Fermi was at the University of Rome, and no one there had ever worked with radioactivity. The laboratory had none of the facilities for atomic bombardment, and very little money for new equipment. Fermi had to make what he needed.

First he had to have a source of neutrons to use as a "gun" for his bombardments. Other scientists had made neutrons by bombarding beryllium with alphas from radium. In Rome radium was out of the question, for it was much too expensive; in Italy at that time it was worth about $34,000 a gram and the University could not afford to buy it.

Fermi, not discouraged, used radon instead; this is the radioactive gas that forms from decaying radium. He mixed radon and beryllium powder in a little glass

Better bullets

tube. This tube was his neutron "gun," but it shot bullets for only a few days; unlike radium, radon decays fast, and its half life is about four days. After that time, the radon in Fermi's glass tube gave off only half the number of alpha particles per second it had given off at first, and it produced only half the number of neutrons per second. Then Fermi had to make new neutron "guns" with fresh radon.

Fermi needed a way of telling whether he was producing radioactivity in the substances he bombarded. The instruments most commonly used to detect radioactivity were, and are, Geiger counters. When a charged particle from a radioactive substance enters a Geiger counter it produces a small electrical discharge, and the counter clicks. Fermi built the Geiger counters that he was to use.

Finally, he needed elements to bombard. He was ambitious and wanted to try all the elements he could lay hands on. He made a list and gave it to his friend Emilio Segré, also a physicist. Segré set off with

Fermi's list and a shopping bag. He went to all the stores that sold chemicals until he had checked off every item that Fermi wanted.

2

When Fermi had what he needed, he started to bombard elements in order, beginning with the element of lowest atomic number, hydrogen, and going on to those of higher atomic number. At first he had no success. Neutrons did not induce radioactivity in hydrogen, beryllium, boron, carbon, or nitrogen. When, after bombarding one of these elements, the young physicist brought it near a Geiger counter, the counter did not click.

Disheartened, Fermi was on the point of giving up neutron bombardment when his luck suddenly changed. Fluorine, the next element he tried, became strongly radioactive, and so did other elements of higher atomic number. This field of research appeared so hopeful that several other young physicists joined Fermi.

Better bullets

Together they went on bombarding elements. Thus they produced many radioactive isotopes that do not exist in nature. Sometimes they obtained a radioactive isotope of the bombarded element. For example, from natural stable sodium they obtained radioactive sodium; from stable iodine and arsenic, they obtained radioactive iodine and arsenic. They also produced radioactive isotopes of different elements. For example, from chlorine they obtained radioactive phosphorus; from silicon, they obtained radioactive aluminum; and from iron, radioactive manganese.

When they bombarded uranium, the element of highest atomic number then known, the results were confusing. They found that in uranium they had produced more than one radioactive element. The amount of each was so exceedingly small that the physicists could not tell with certainty what elements they had produced.

In all previous atomic bombardments, the bombarded element had changed into an isotope of an element of close atomic number. Thus, for instance, iron,

The Story of Atomic Energy

of atomic number 26, had changed into an isotope of manganese, of atomic number 25. But the group in Rome found that at least one of the radioactive products of uranium was not an isotope of any known element close to uranium. They had reason to believe they had perhaps made a *new element,* of atomic number 93, which does not exist in nature. They thought they had made element 93, but they were not sure and did not find a way of making sure.

These doubts about element 93 are an example of the difficulties that scientists meet when they explore a new field. The physicists in Rome did not have our modern equipment or the deeper understanding of radioactive atoms that their own studies, and those of others, have helped us to gain. No one among them had yet become sufficiently skilled in handling radioactive substances to separate the extremely tiny amount of the mysterious element from the other radioactive products of uranium.

Fermi realized that he and his group could not hope to identify the products of uranium unless they gained

Better bullets

greater skill and learned more about the ways in which neutrons act on atoms. Accordingly, they went back to bombarding elements other than uranium and to studying more closely what happens to these elements when neutrons hit them. In the course of their experiments they made an interesting discovery.

3

One day the physicists in Rome were bombarding a piece of silver with neutrons. To their surprise they found that the radioactivity produced was not always the same. At times their piece of silver might give off one hundred beta particles per minute, at other times only eighty. They soon found that they could change the activity of the silver by placing different objects between it and their neutron "gun." A plate of lead, for instance, placed between the neutron source and the piece of silver made the activity increase slightly.

At first the changes produced in the radioactivity of the piece of silver were not very great. Then one morn-

The Story of Atomic Energy

ing the physicists placed a large piece of paraffin between the neutron source and the silver. When they brought the silver to a Geiger counter to measure its activity, the counter clicked madly. Paraffin increased the radioactivity of silver up to one hundred times.

Amazed, the physicists shouted to one another: "Fantastic! Incredible! Black magic!"

In the afternoon Fermi suggested a more realistic explanation. Paraffin contains a great amount of hydrogen, he said. Hydrogen nuclei are protons, which have the same mass as neutrons. When paraffin is placed between the neutron source and a piece of silver, the neutrons from the source go through the paraffin before reaching the silver. In the paraffin the neutrons hit many protons. As a result, they are slowed down, just as billiard balls are slowed down when they hit other billiard balls of the same size.

These *slow* neutrons, Fermi said, have a much better chance than fast neutrons of being captured by silver nuclei, just as slow balls are caught more easily and in larger numbers by ballplayers than balls that zoom by at great speed. The result is that a greater number of silver nuclei can each capture a neutron, break down, and become radioactive.

Fermi was not certain that his explanation was correct—that the great increase in the activity of silver was due to the fact that the hydrogen in the paraffin slowed down neutrons. But he reasoned that if his explanation *was* correct, any other substance containing a great amount of hydrogen—water, for example—should have the same effect as paraffin.

The physicists decided to make the test. The simplest way of doing it with water was to immerse a neutron source and silver in it, but keep them at some distance, so that the neutrons from the source would have a chance of hitting many hydrogen nuclei and of being greatly slowed down before reaching the silver. To do this the physicists needed a large amount of water. Because they were too excited to wait until they had found a large container, they decided to do their experiment in the goldfish fountain in the back yard of the physics building.

The Story of Atomic Energy

At that time the University of Rome was not on a campus, as it is now; its buildings were scattered about town. The physics and chemistry buildings had been sisters' convents in the past. They were on hilly ground among bamboo and palm trees, near ancient churches and bell towers. Modern buildings are better suited for modern laboratories, but remodeled convents with goldfish fountains make for pleasanter surroundings.

Fermi and his friends rushed to plunge their neutron "gun" and piece of silver into the goldfish fountain. The fish, of course, stayed calm and silent, but the men shouted in excitement. Water increased the radioactivity of silver as much as paraffin did. This was an important corroboration of Fermi's explanation.

The physicists in Rome would have been even more excited had they foreseen that slow neutrons were to play an important role in the production of atomic energy for the benefit of mankind.

5

The riddle of element 93

1

When Fermi and his group in Rome bombarded uranium with neutrons and found the mysterious substance that they suspected to be element 93, the news spread rapidly. The idea that men might have created an element that did not exist before caught the imagination of many people. Some newspapers wrote of element 93 as if there were no doubts about it. The New York *Times*, for instance, published an article in two columns under a large heading: "Italian Produces 93rd

Element by Bombarding Uranium." (It is easy to imagine the surprise of readers who had never heard of atomic bullets and who were learning that a bombardment had created an element!)

Scientists all over the world began discussing whether or not the news could be true. Many did not believe that the physicists in Rome had really created an element. Although Fermi had said that his mysterious substance was not one of the elements close to uranium—like, for instance, element 91—some physicists suggested that the new substance was an isotope of protoactinium, which is element 91.

This suggestion keenly interested a team of workers at the Kaiser Wilhelm Institute in Berlin: the German chemist Otto Hahn and the Austrian woman physicist Lise Meitner. Almost twenty years earlier this team had discovered protoactinium, and had studied its chemical properties. They knew it well and were confident that they could recognize it easily.

As a young graduate, Otto Hahn had studied and

The riddle of element 93

worked with Ernest Rutherford in Montreal, Canada. Hahn had learned to handle and isolate tiny amounts of radioactive substances and to recognize their properties. Radiochemistry had become his career.

Shortly after Hahn's return from Canada to Berlin, Lise Meitner had gone to see him in his laboratory. She told him that she was on a short visit from Vienna. But her "short visit" lasted more than thirty years; she found Hahn's work so interesting that she changed her plans, accepted a position in Berlin, and became Hahn's collaborator. Otto Hahn and Lise Meitner were not only experts in protoactinium, they were also among the most skilled workers in the special methods used in radioactivity.

This experienced team set about repeating Fermi's experiments. They bombarded uranium with slow neutrons; then they examined the substances that had formed from uranium. There was no protoactinium. This gave strength to Fermi's findings, including his suggestion that the mysterious product might be element 93. Yet the problem of understanding what happened to uranium atoms when they were hit by neutrons became more and more puzzling.

Among the products of uranium bombardment, Hahn and Meitner found a larger number of substances than Fermi had. Although they always produced these substances in amounts too small to be seen, they could identify them with Geiger counters. Each substance had a different half life.

Over a period of several years Otto Hahn and Lise Meitner went on bombarding uranium and studying its radioactive products. Another chemist, Fritz Strassmann, joined them. For a long time they believed that all these products were *transuranic* elements. (Transuranic is a name given to elements of higher atomic numbers than uranium.) In other words, they thought that they had created not only element 93, but also elements 94 and 95, and perhaps others. They also determined some general chemical properties of this transuranic group of elements.

Then, in 1938, they learned that Irene Joliot-Curie

The riddle of element 93

and a co-worker in Paris had found a new transuranic substance among the products of uranium bombardment. This substance did not fit into the general picture of transuranic elements. Hahn, Meitner, and Strassmann planned to repeat the experiments of Irene Joliot and her co-worker and to check the results. But at about this time Lise Meitner had to give up her work and leave Germany.

2

From now on our story becomes complicated by historical events of a different nature. The dictator Adolf Hitler and his Nazi party were ruling Germany. The Nazis did not believe in democracy, and they governed by force, imposing their will on all Germans. Under the Nazis there was no freedom. Hitler and his party decided what political views people should have, what the press and radio should say, what the teachers should teach, and what children should do in their spare time. Adults and children were drilled as soldiers, because Hitler and his party wanted to conquer Europe.

Without freedom science cannot live. Scientists are used to thinking, to discussing their views with others, to choosing what they want to study or to teach. But Hitler was determined to change all this. Scientists who expressed views that were different from Hitler's lost their positions. In addition, Hitler hated and persecuted all Jews. As a result, many German scientists, especially those of Jewish background, left Germany.

In July, 1938, the Nazi persecution reached Lise Meitner. Warned by friends, she managed to escape from Germany and to find safety in Stockholm, Sweden. Her collaboration with Otto Hahn, which had lasted over thirty years, came suddenly to an end.

Hahn and Strassmann carried on without Meitner the work that had been started in her company. When the two men repeated Irene Joliot's experiments, they found a substance with chemical properties similar to those of radium. At first they thought that it *was* radium.

The riddle of element 93

Then the two scientists tried to isolate this radium from the transuranic elements. They followed a method that Hahn had successfully used in the past. To the products of uranium bombardment they added some barium, a metal with chemical properties similar to those of radium. In a solution, barium drags radium along and the two elements precipitate together. Then radium and barium can be separated.

But in spite of their efforts, Hahn and Strassmann could not separate from the barium the substance they thought to be radium. They began to have doubts about this radium of theirs. At one time they called it "curiosium" because it showed very curious properties.

They checked and rechecked their results several times. Finally, they came to the conclusion that they could not separate *their* "curiosium" from barium for the simple reason that it *was* barium.

This discovery was puzzling. How could barium have formed from uranium? The atomic number of uranium is 92, and its atomic mass is 238. The atomic number of barium is 56 and the atomic mass of the barium in Hahn and Strassmann's experiment is 139.

Hahn and Strassmann were chemists, and only physicists can determine how radioactive atoms will decay. When Hahn had spoken to physicists about the radium that he thought he had produced from uranium, they had told him that he must have made a mistake. The atomic number of radium is 88, too far removed from the 92 of uranium. It seemed impossible to them that a particle as small as a neutron could make an atom give off enough particles to account for the loss of four electric charges. What would the physicists say now when they learned that barium was found in the products of uranium bombardment? The atomic number of barium is little more than half that of uranium!

Hahn and Strassmann prepared a paper for a German scientific journal, in which they related these "experiments that are at variance with all previous experiences in nuclear physics." They had no doubts about their results, yet they expressed themselves with caution. As chemists they hesitated to announce a discovery which at that time went against all the rules of physics.

3

Hahn wrote to Lise Meitner, informing her of the discovery of barium in the products of uranium bombardment. His letter reached her before the scientific paper was published, and thus Lise Meitner became the first scientist outside Germany to learn of Hahn's and Strassmann's discovery. She realized what had happened—some uranium atoms had split into two almost equal parts. (The other part was identified shortly afterwards; it was a rare gas, krypton, of atomic number 36. This 36, plus 56, the atomic number of barium, equals 92, the atomic number of uranium.)

Lise Meitner gave the name of *fission* to this new phenomenon, the splitting in two of uranium atoms. It seemed to her that it was similar to the division in two of living cells, which biologists call fission. She thought

The Story of Atomic Energy

that when uranium split into two almost equal pieces an enormous amount of energy might be released and that the two pieces might fly apart with tremendous speed.

Since the early days of radioactivity, physicists had asked themselves whether it would ever be possible to "unlock the store of energy" in atoms. Perhaps Lise Meitner guessed that fission was to be the key that would "unlock" that store of energy. The fact is that she felt she could not possibly keep the knowledge of Hahn's and Strassmann's discovery to herself.

It was during the Christmas vacation when Hahn's letter reached her, and Lise happened to be visiting with friends in a small Swedish village. In the group there was another physicist, her young nephew Otto Frisch, who had also escaped from Germany because of Hitler's persecution. Lise talked to him about Hahn's letter, but at first Otto would not believe that uranium atoms could split into two almost equal chunks. He thought that Hahn and Strassmann must have made a mistake.

* 54 *

The riddle of element 93

In order to talk the matter over at leisure, the aunt and nephew took a long walk in the snow. Physical exercise, they thought, might clear their minds. Lise Meitner did most of the talking, urgently, convincingly. At last she persuaded Otto that Hahn and Strassmann had made no mistake, that uranium atoms underwent fission, and that the energy released in the process was probably very great.

Once he became convinced, Otto Frisch felt, like his aunt, that they should not keep the news of fission to themselves. They decided to inform Niels Bohr at once. Bohr, whom we have already mentioned briefly, had done so much to explain the nature of atoms and why atoms behave as they do that he was considered the greatest living atomic physicist. (Ernest Rutherford had died the year before.)

Bohr lived in Copenhagen, Denmark, and so aunt and nephew hastened to that city. They found Bohr on the point of leaving for a stay of several months in the United States, where he was going to visit his friend, the world's most famous physicist, Albert Einstein. Einstein had left his home in Germany when Hitler had risen to power and was living in Princeton, New Jersey.

Lise Meitner and Otto Frisch arrived in Copenhagen just in time to talk briefly with Bohr. He listened eagerly, discussed fission with them, and suggested an experiment by which they might measure the energy released when uranium atoms split. He was so engrossed in this new, extraordinary phenomenon, fission, that he almost missed the train to his ship.

Bohr had the reputation of being absent-minded, but under similar circumstances the least absent-minded physicist might have missed a train. To a scientist, there is no greater pleasure than to learn of one of those rare discoveries that, like fission, are "at variance with all previous experiences." Such discoveries reveal new ways in which nature works and open new paths to learning. Scientists like to guess where these new paths will lead.

John Dalton

(1766–1844)

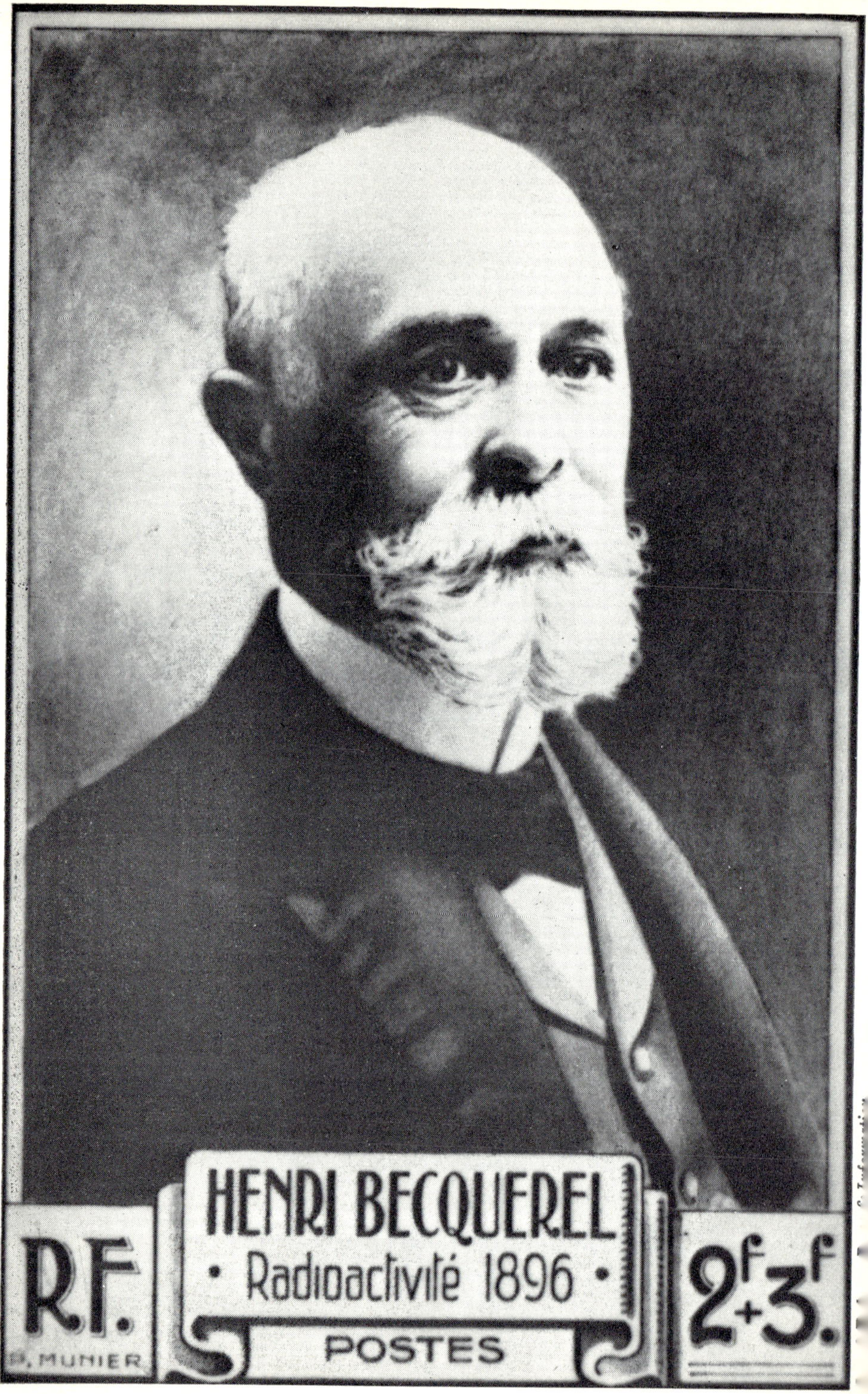
HENRI BECQUEREL
• Radioactivité 1896 •
POSTES
R.F.
MUNIER
2f +3f.

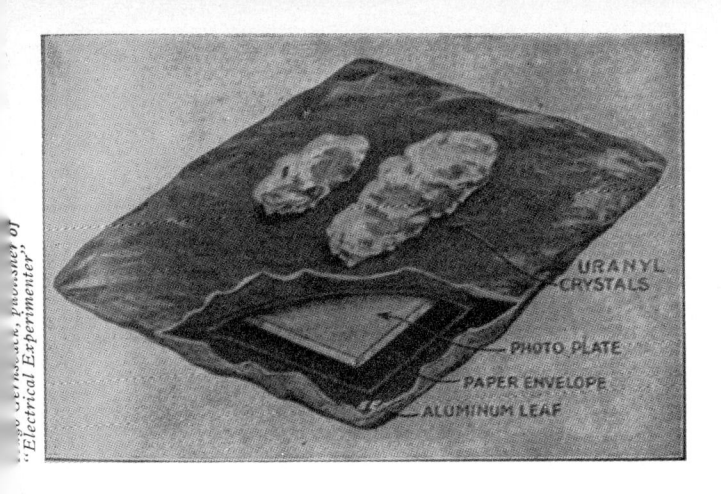

(Left) Henri Becquerel

(Above) How Becquerel performed his historic experiment. A photographic plate was wrapped in black paper, then in aluminum foil. Uranyl crystals were placed on top. The result is shown in the illustration below. *(Below)* Photographic plate showing the first evidence of radioactivity sought by Becquerel.

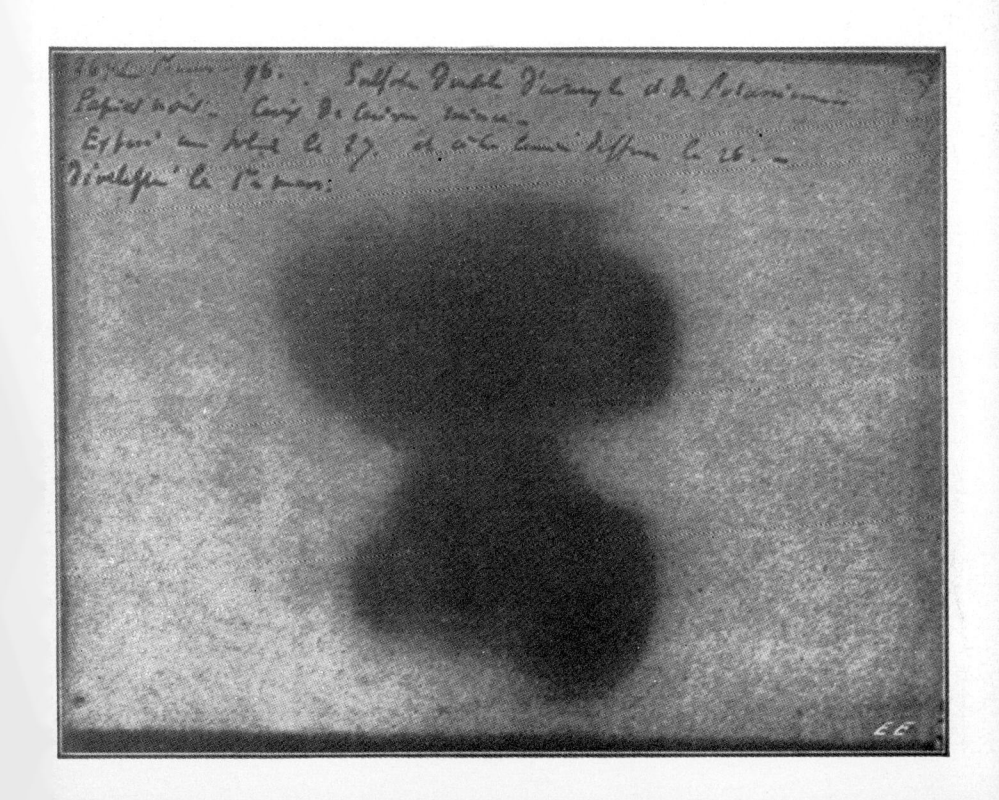

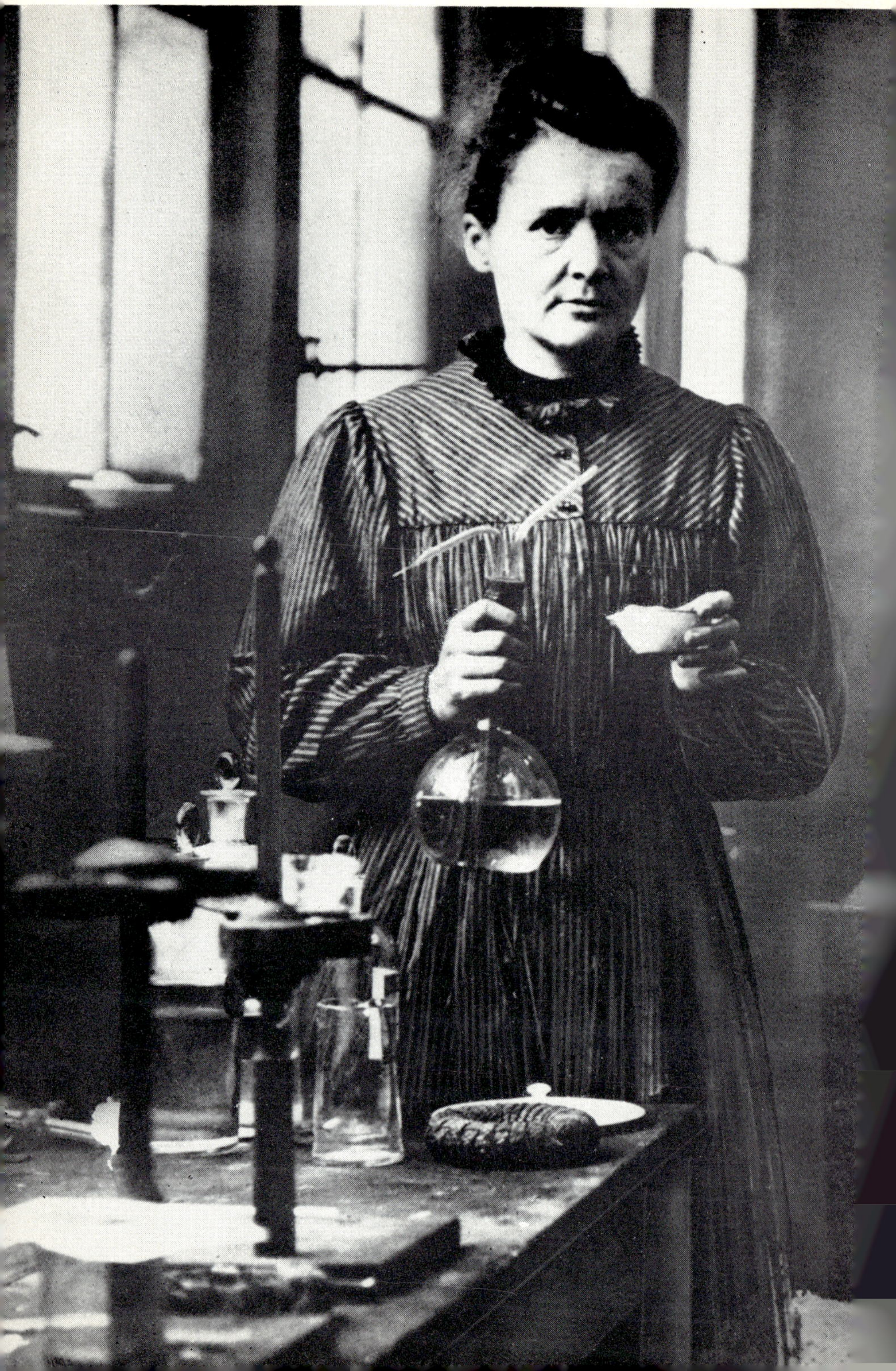

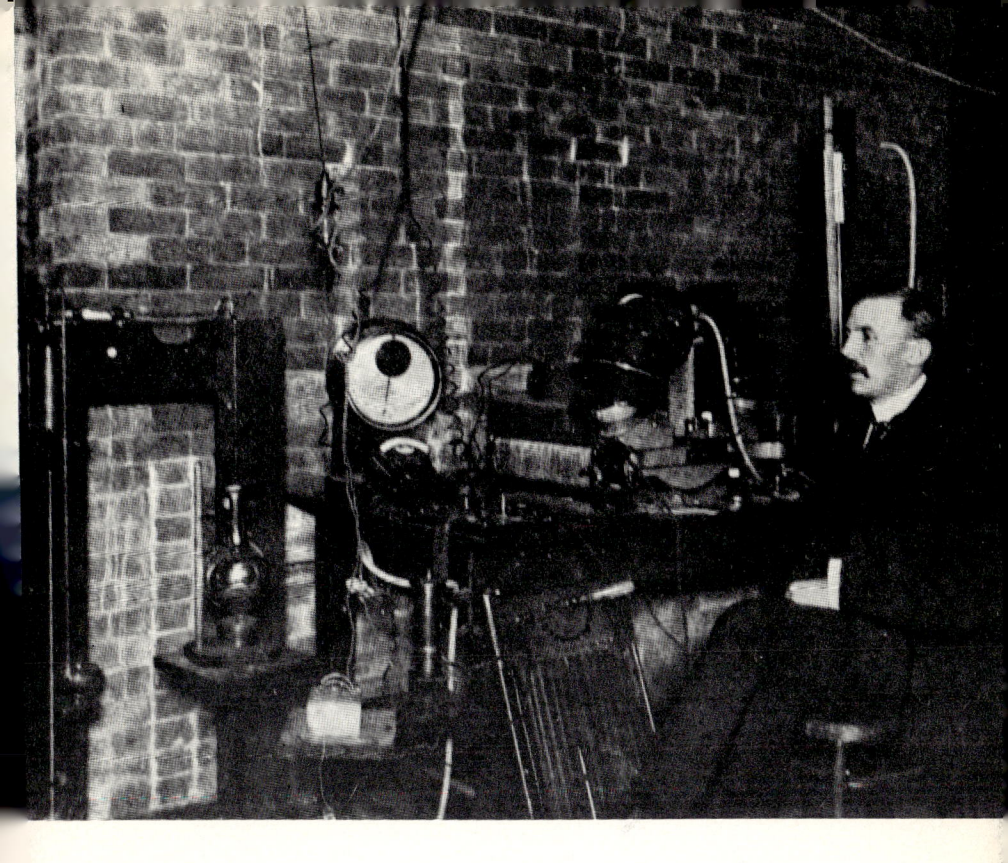

Ernest Rutherford in 1905, at McGill University in Montreal, Canada.

(Left) Madame Curie, shown in her laboratory.

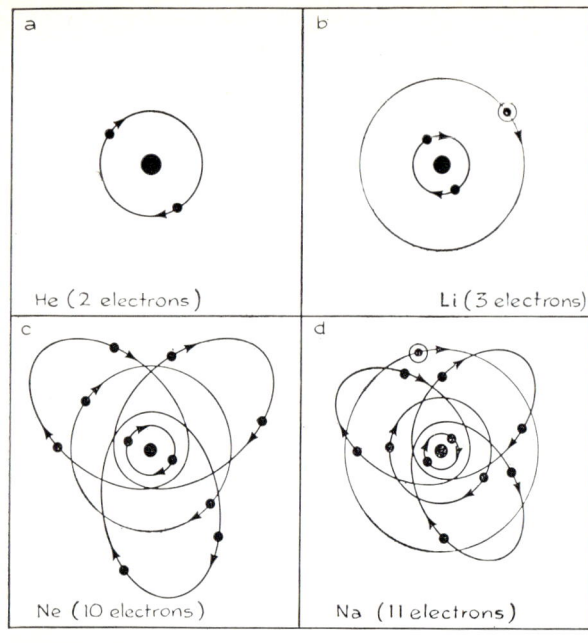

Models of atoms showing the orbits of electrons around the nucleus. Top: helium, lithium, neon, sodium. Bottom: uranium. In reality electrons and nuclei are *not* well defined little balls; rather, the electrons form some sort of cloud around the nucleus.

Adapted from Gamow, "Matter, Earth and Sky" (Prentice-Hall, Inc. 1958)

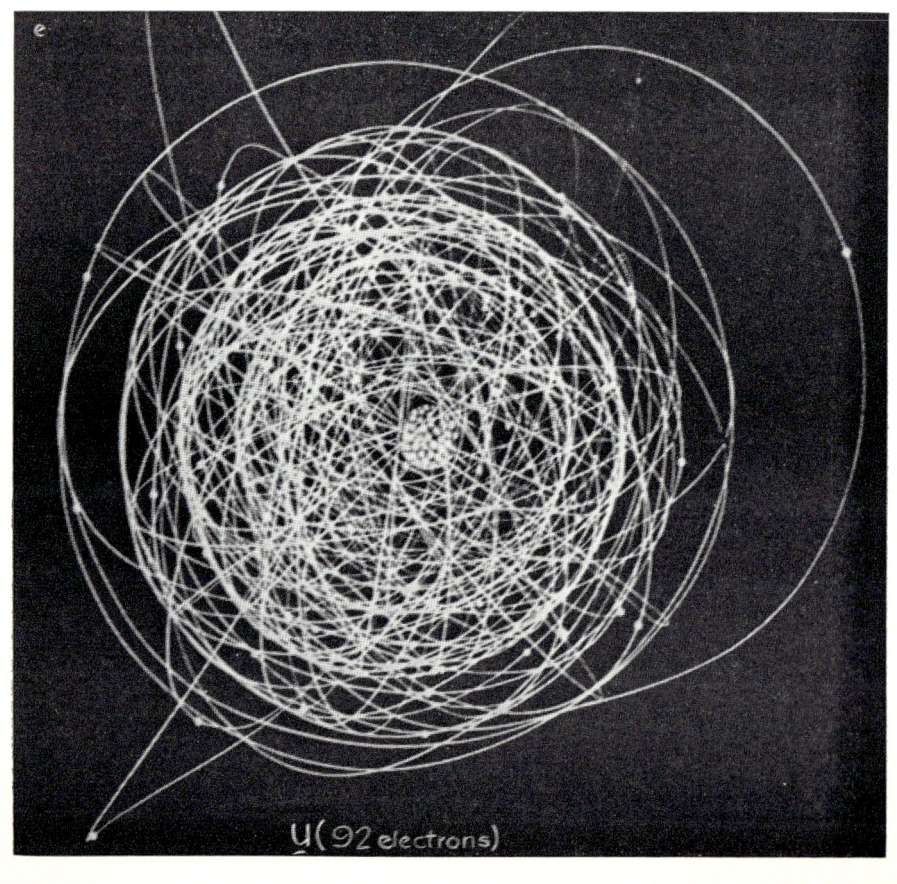

In a Wilson cloud chamber small droplets of fog condense along the paths of charged particles and so the paths can be photographed. Top: Paths of alpha particles from polonium. Bottom: Paths of alpha particles in nitrogen. The two forks are each due to the disintegration of an atom of nitrogen: the heavy branch is the path of an atom of oxygen, the light branch of a proton.

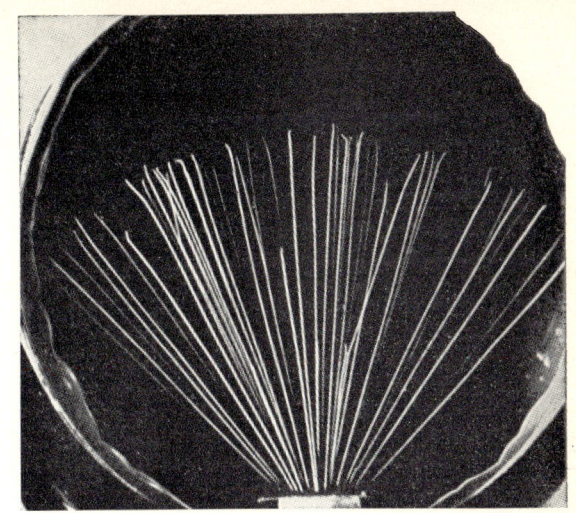

(Blackett)

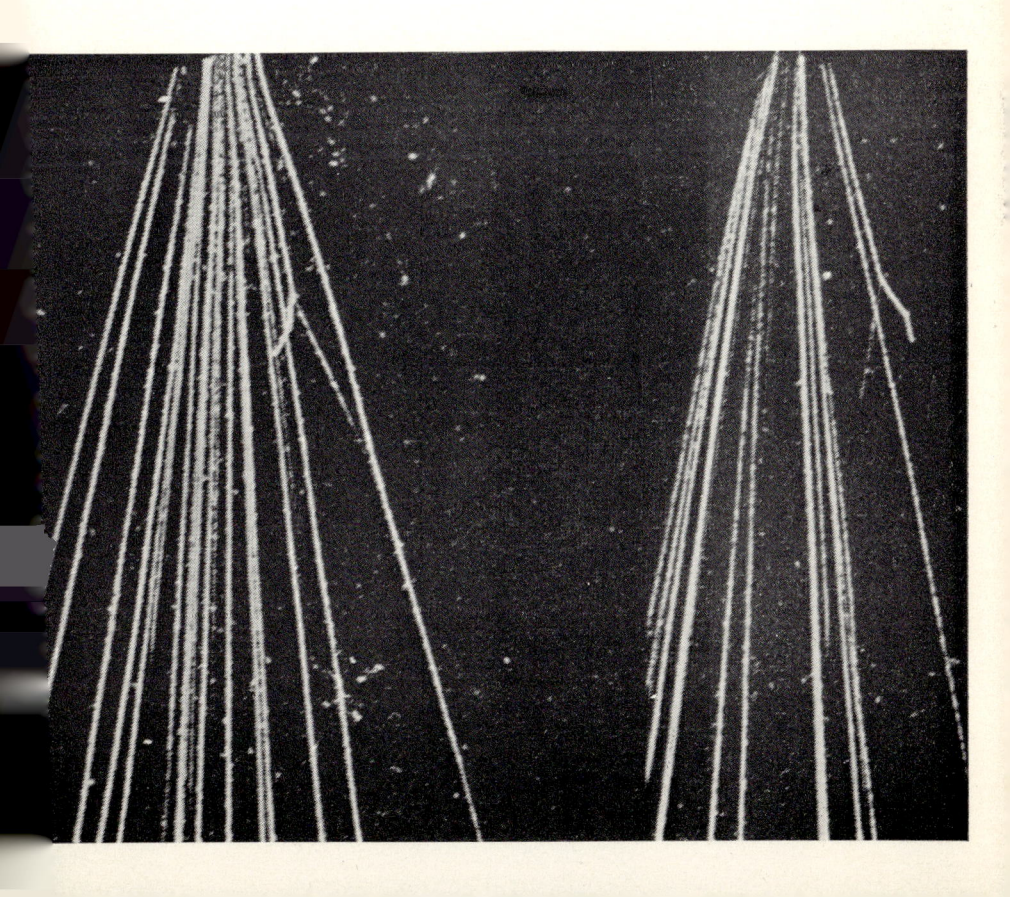

Enrico Fermi and Emilio Segré.

(Left) About 1930: A laboratory in the Physics Building in Rome.

Twenty years later: the giant cyclotron in Chicago.

Reprinted from Atoms in the Family by Laura Fermi by permission of the University of Chicago Press.

From Foundations of Modern Physical Science, by Gerald Holton and Duane H. D. Roller, 1958, Addison-Wesley, Reading, Mass.

Otto Hahn and Lise Meitner in their laboratory.

Artist's conception of the first atomic pile.

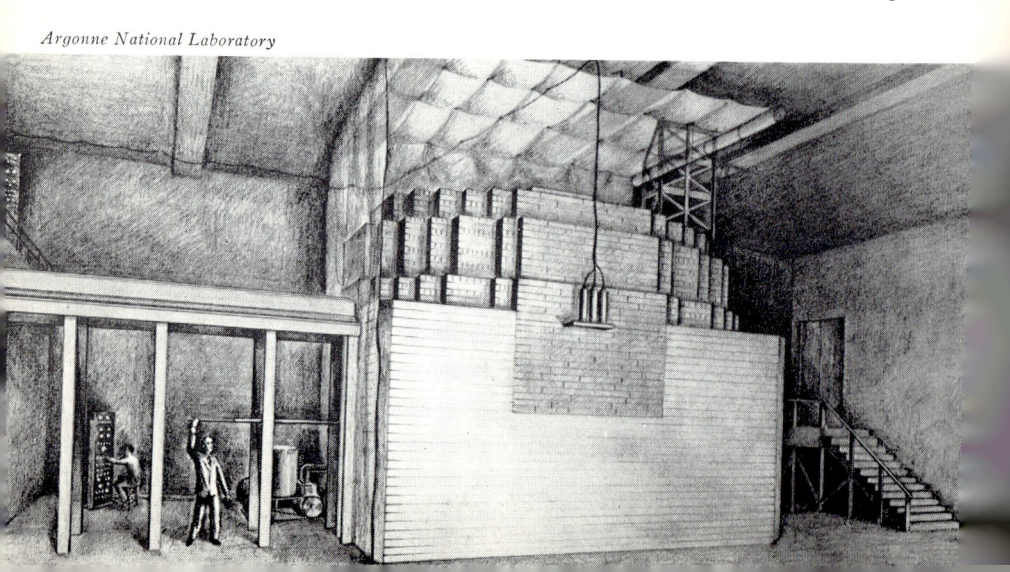

Argonne National Laboratory

Nuclear weapon of the type detonated over Hiroshima, Japan, in World War II. The bomb is 28 inches in diameter and 120 inches long. The first nuclear weapon ever detonated, it weighed about 9,000 pounds and had a yield equivalent to approximately 20,000 tons of high explosive.

Los Alamos Scientific Laboratory

An aerial view of one of the production plants at the Clinton Engineer Works at Oak Ridge, Tennessee.

U.S. Army photo

Johnson, Richland, Washington

One of the original chemical separation plants, built at Richland, Washington, during World War II to extract plutonium from the material discharged from the reactors. Stack for discharge of waste gases is 200 feet high.

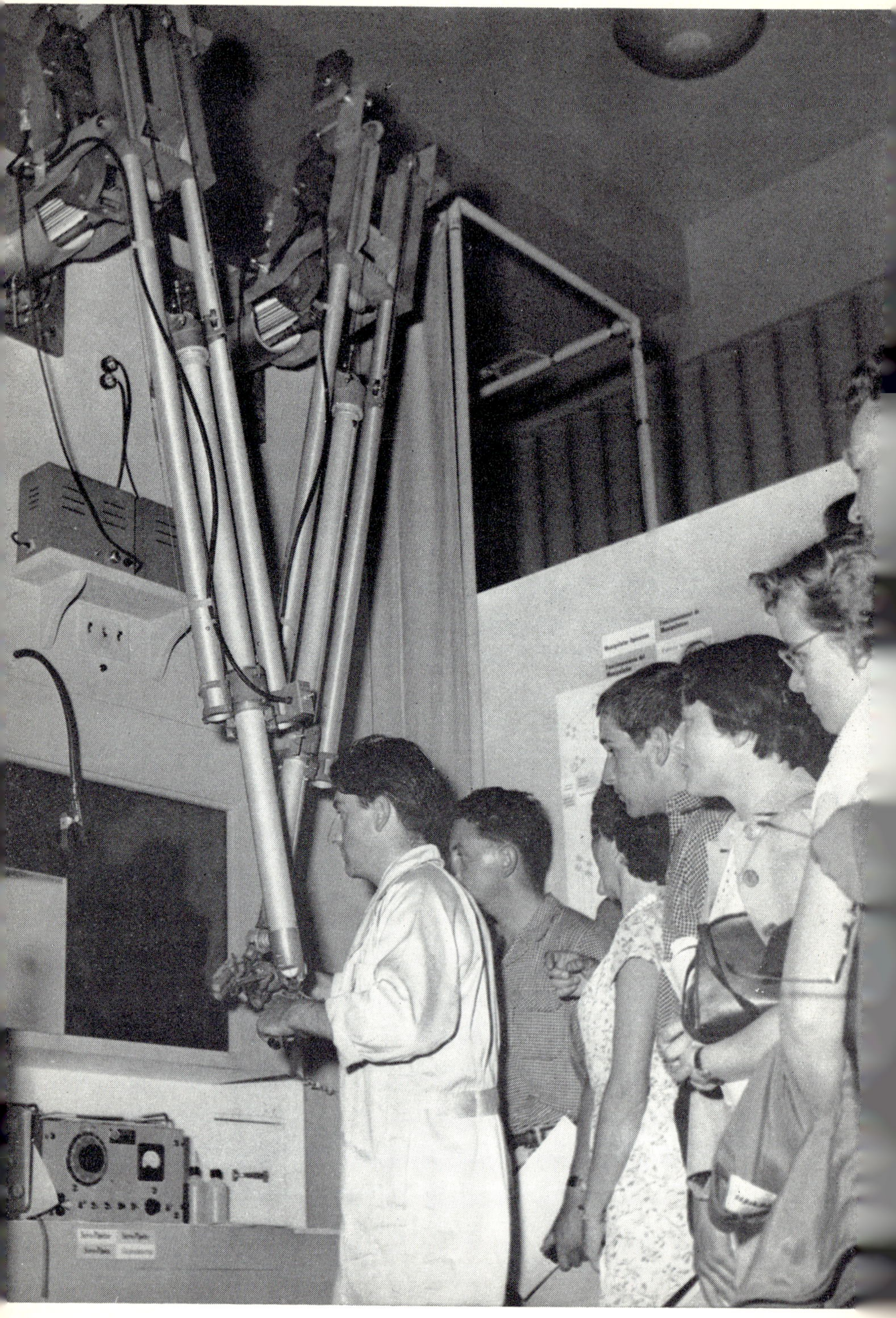

(Left) Visitors to the United States Atomic exhibition at Geneva watch the "magic hands" at work on a modern nuclear reactor.

Simple apparatus with which fission of uranium was discovered.

Commonwealth Edison Company's Dresden Nuclear Power Station located 50 miles southwest of Chicago. This 180,000 kilowatt station went into commercial operation in August, 1960.

The riddle of element 93

4

Now our story will move away from Europe and across the ocean along with Bohr's ship. Studies of the atom had gone on in other parts of the world, including the United States. Yet many of the most important discoveries were made in Europe. Our brief survey of them has taken us to ancient Greece, England, France, Germany, Denmark, Italy, and only briefly outside Europe, to Canada, where we followed Rutherford. But from now on most of our story will take place in the United States.

When Bohr sailed for the United States in early January, 1939, Hitler was becoming more and more aggressive, and the Second World War was approaching. Many German scientists had left their country, and great numbers were also fleeing Italy, Poland, Hungary, and other countries that had fallen under Hitler's influence or were threatened by him.

Many of the best European scientists came to the

The Story of Atomic Energy

United States. So, while science in Europe was losing ground, it was gaining in the United States. Hitler was giving his enemies a great advantage, but he did not realize it!

Among the physicists who came to the United States were Enrico Fermi and a few of the friends who had worked with him in Rome. Like Germany, Italy was then ruled by a dictator, Benito Mussolini, and his Fascist party. For several years Mussolini had not been as bad a dictator as Hitler, but now he was falling more and more under Hitler's influence. In the end, lack of freedom drove Fermi and some of his friends out of Italy.

Fermi arrived in New York only two weeks before Bohr, and became a professor at Columbia University.

While Bohr was crossing the ocean, Meitner and Frisch were at work back in Europe. By the time Bohr arrived in Princeton, Lise Meitner and Otto Frisch had already performed the experiment that Bohr had suggested before leaving Copenhagen; they had measured the energy that uranium freed when it split into two

The riddle of element 93

big, almost equal chunks. As they had predicted, the released energy was very great.

The scientists in the United States had not learned of fission before Bohr's arrival; there had not been enough time. After Bohr's arrival in Princeton, the news of fission spread rapidly to many universities.

When Fermi learned about it he finally understood what had happened when he and his friends had bombarded uranium with neutrons. They had produced fission but had not recognized it. They did not have enough imagination and it did not occur to them that uranium might break in a different way from other elements. They had known that their product was not an element of atomic mass and number close to uranium but had never thought of looking for elements close to barium.

When uranium atoms undergo fission, they may break in slightly different ways, forming several elements of atomic mass and number about half those of uranium. "What at that time we thought might be element 93," Fermi said, "has proved to be a mixture

The Story of Atomic Energy

of decay products. We had suspected it for a long time, now we are sure of it. We thought that we had a mixture of four elements while their number was closer to fifty." His element 93 and the transuranic elements of the Berlin workers were fission products.

Although this is not the very end of the story of element 93, for the moment we may consider that the riddle was solved.

6

Uranium and the Second World War

1

It occurred to several physicists that when uranium atoms split in two they might give off neutrons. This idea seemed so exciting that at once many physicists set themselves to look for neutrons in fission. But why was this idea exciting? Why look for neutrons? What did it matter whether or not neutrons were produced in fission? What could physicists do with them?

The fact is that physicists had a new thought: Perhaps fission could make it possible to use the energy

The Story of Atomic Energy

stored in the atoms. In the past this had seemed impossible to many people. After having broken atoms for fourteen years, Rutherford once said: ". . . we cannot control atomic energy to an extent which would be of any value commercially, and I believe we are not likely ever to be able to do so." But now it looked as if fission could be the key that would unlock the store of energy in atoms, and that neutrons could do the job.

Physicists reasoned this way: It takes one neutron to split one atom of uranium, and *we must make* that neutron. (Remember Fermi's neutron "guns.") Let us suppose, the physicists thought, that when a uranium atom splits in two it gives off two neutrons. We would now have two neutrons, without having to make them. These two neutrons might hit two more uranium atoms, split them, and make them give off two neutrons each. At the end of this second step we would have four neutrons, which might split four more atoms. If these gave off two neutrons each, we would then have eight neutrons which might split eight atoms. Fission of uranium might then go on by itself in a

Uranium and the Second World War

chain reaction. At each step the number of neutrons would double. In a very short time, the physicists concluded, a huge number of uranium atoms would split.

The importance of a chain reaction lies in the fact that each splitting atom gives off energy. We have said several times that this energy is very great. In reality, for all practical purposes the amount of energy that a single atom gives off is very small. But in a chain reaction so many atoms would split that the total amount of energy would be very large. If all atoms in one ounce of uranium were to split, they would free enough energy to keep twenty thousand common electric bulbs lighted for about twelve days.

We can well understand why the physicists wanted to know whether or not uranium atoms gave off neutrons when they split!

2

In 1939, the physicists in the United States who set themselves to look for neutrons in fission had more

The Story of Atomic Energy

powerful bullets for their bombardments—and a greater quantity of them—than the scientists in Europe had ever had.

From the time when Rutherford had first bombarded atoms with alpha particles, physicists had wanted more and better bullets than those that come spontaneously from radioactive substances. They had thought they might use protons; hydrogen nuclei are protons, and hydrogen is plentiful. But hydrogen nuclei do not move fast, like the particles from radioactive nuclei, and they do not have enough energy to hit and break atoms. Scientists planned machines to speed up protons and other particles. These machines are now called *accelerators*.

When Fermi arrived in the United States, he found that at Columbia University there was a type of accelerator called a *cyclotron*. A few years before, a California physicist, Ernest O. Lawrence, had invented and built the first cyclotron in Berkeley, California.

The essential parts of a cyclotron are a large mag-

Uranium and the Second World War

net and a metal box. (Modern cyclotrons have huge magnets: the one now in use at the University of California has a magnet that weighs four thousand tons.) The metal box is placed between the two poles of the magnet, and protons or other charged particles are sent inside it. An electric field gives the particles a series of small pushes, and at each push their speed becomes a little greater. If the magnet were not there, the particles would fly away in a straight line and would be out of reach before they could gain much speed. The magnet bends their path and makes them stay inside the box, where the particles go round and round, faster and faster, until in the end they come out with very great speed and energy.

Fermi was very happy to be able to use the cyclotron at Columbia University. He could speed up particles in it, and direct them against a piece of beryllium, thus producing a large number of neutrons. In this way he could have about 100,000 more neutrons per second than he could have had with one of his neutron

The Story of Atomic Energy

guns in Rome. He could break many more uranium atoms, and this made it easier for him to see what happened when they broke.

Very soon Fermi and many other physicists, both at Columbia and at other universities, found that uranium atoms did give off neutrons when they split. This was an important piece of news that changed the outlook on unlocking the store of energy in the atoms. But was it good or bad news? At the moment it seemed bad. Fission had been discovered in Germany, Hitler's country. A war appeared more and more likely. Would the Germans be able to use atomic energy for war ends? Would they be able to run their battleships with atomic power or, even worse, to produce some sort of atomic explosion?

There was still hope that, although a chain reaction was possible in theory, it would be impossible in practice. When physicists had produced fission in their laboratories, fission had not caused a chain reaction; most of the neutrons that uranium gave off when splitting fled away from the uranium or were lost for other reasons. Too few neutrons hit and broke uranium atoms. Perhaps it would never be possible to cause a very large number of neutrons to break atoms of uranium. The only way of knowing whether a chain reaction was possible was to try.

Many scientists felt that they should not waste their time on something that was perhaps impossible, and they gave up research on fission. But the physicists at Columbia University went on stubbornly.

3

The physicists who had recently come from Europe were worried. They knew that fission had been discovered in Germany; they also knew the ways of dictators. They were afraid that Hitler might have ordered all German scientists to work on fission, the chain reaction, and its use in war. Perhaps the Germans were already planning to make atomic weapons.

The physicists from Europe felt that someone in our

The Story of Atomic Energy

government should know of fission and of what fission might do in a war. With this in mind Fermi went to see an admiral in Washington. In his thick Italian accent (he had arrived only two and a half months before) he said that perhaps . . . under certain circumstances . . . scientists might make uranium explode. The explosion of a pound of uranium would be a million times more powerful than the explosion of a pound of any known explosive, Fermi said. But he was not at all sure that such an explosion would ever take place in uranium.

It is likely that the admiral was puzzled. What could he do if the physicists themselves did not know whether this explosion was possible? Nothing much came of Fermi's talk.

The scientists did not give up. The next attempt to alert the United States government to the dangers of atomic explosions was made by two Hungarian physicists, Leo Szilard and Eugene Wigner, and this time it was successful. Leo Szilard was working at Columbia with Fermi; Eugene Wigner was teaching in

Uranium and the Second World War

Princeton and had become interested in the theoretical aspects of fission. The two Hungarians were more worried than anyone else about atomic explosions. Wigner thought a great deal about what he could do, talked with many friends, and decided on a plan of action. He persuaded Szilard to go with him to see Einstein in Princeton.

Wigner and Szilard had several good reasons for wanting to make this visit. Einstein was by far the best-known scientist in the United States, and the government would probably accept his opinion. He had been born in Germany and still had friends there; it was possible that he had an idea of how far the Germans had gone in research on fission and the chain reaction.

Einstein was certainly interested in fission. Years earlier he had said that mass can change into energy, and energy into mass; that every time some mass seems lost, some energy is created. He had also written a formula to calculate how much energy is created when a certain mass is lost.

The Story of Atomic Energy

Fission could provide a striking proof that Einstein's formula was correct; physicists had used Einstein's formula to calculate how much energy should be freed in fission. Then in their laboratories they had measured the freed energy. Both times they had obtained the same figures!

Undoubtedly Einstein was the best person to act as a link between scientists and government. Wigner and Szilard talked with him a long time, and in the end it was decided that Einstein's two visitors would prepare a letter to President Roosevelt and that Einstein would sign it.

When the letter was ready Wigner and Szilard took it to Einstein, who read the words to which he was to put his name:

"Some recent work by E. Fermi and L. Szilard . . . leads me to expect that the element uranium may be turned into a new and important source of energy in the immediate future . . . it may become possible to set up a nuclear chain reaction in a large mass of uranium, by which vast amounts of power . . . would be

Uranium and the Second World War

generated. . . . This new phenomenon would also lead to the construction of bombs, and it is conceivable—though much less certain—that extremely powerful bombs of a new type may thus be constructed. . . ."

The letter was two full typewritten pages. It stated also that the Germans were doing research on fission in one of their best laboratories and that the Nazis had stopped selling uranium to other countries in order to keep it all for themselves. This was a serious warning to the United States government.

When Einstein reached the end of the letter he said: "For the first time in history men will use energy that does not come from the sun." Then he signed the letter. It was August 2, 1939.

Einsten, Wigner, and Szilard decided that the letter should not go through the mails. A friend of Szilard's agreed to deliver the letter to the President, but he could not get an immediate appointment.

Then on September 1, the Second World War broke out in Europe. On October 11, President Roosevelt received Einstein's letter from the hands of Szilard's friend. At once the President appointed an "Advisory Committee on Uranium." This committee was to keep in touch with the scientists and report to the President.

At Szilard's suggestion, atomic physicists in the United States took another step. They agreed, of their own free will, to keep secret all studies on fission and the chain reaction. Usually scientists believe that secrecy is bad for science and that their findings belong to all men. Under normal circumstances they would never have suggested secrecy. On the other hand, they believed that Hitler and the Nazis had to be defeated if freedom and the democratic way of life were to survive. Information on the chain reaction might help Hitler win the war. Secrecy was necessary. So the lid of secrecy fell on all atomic research in the United States.

7

Birth of the atomic age

1

The "Advisory Committee on Uranium" was a link between physicists and government, but for a while it did not change matters. Physicists were vague and uncertain when they talked of atomic energy, and the government had no reason for vigorous action. The group at Columbia University remained small and went on working with only the means that had been theirs before the Committee was established.

In the small group at Columbia, Szilard and Fermi

The Story of Atomic Energy

remained the leaders, and the pace of their research never slackened. They knew they would have to overcome very great difficulties before they could even hope to achieve a chain reaction. One of their main difficulties was the quality of their bullets; the neutrons that uranium gave off in fission were too fast, and even when they hit uranium atoms they did not often make these atoms split. Neutrons from fission were indeed poor bullets.

Another difficulty was the number of bullets that did not do their duty but went astray. Under normal conditions most neutrons ran out into the air or were captured by matter before they had a chance of hitting uranium atoms.

Fermi and Szilard knew they had to slow down neutrons and see whether they could make more neutrons stay inside uranium and produce fission. They were not sure that this could be done, even though slowing down neutrons was an old trick for Fermi—it went back to the time when he and his friends had plunged their neutron "gun" and a piece of silver in the gold-

* 74 *

fish fountain in Rome. Now he and his group at Columbia University undertook the study of fission under water. After several months of research, they came to the conclusion that water, paraffin, and other substances that contain hydrogen are not satisfactory for a chain reaction; hydrogen absorbs too many neutrons. To achieve a chain reaction they would have to slow down neutrons with some other substance, and they eventually reached the decision to use carbon, in the form of graphite.

Fermi and Szilard planned to pile up layers of graphite and alternate them with layers of graphite containing chunks of uranium. Their pile would have to be very large and bulky, for if it were small, neutrons would escape before they had a chance of producing fission. No one knew how large a "very large and bulky" pile would be.

To make a large pile the physicists needed great quantities of uranium and graphite, and this presented another difficulty, for only very pure graphite and pure uranium metal—not its compounds—could be used. But uranium mines yield nothing but uranium compounds, and in the United States only tiny amounts of pure uranium metal had been separated—less than an ounce.

Graphite for a pile had to be extremely pure because impurities have an amazing power to capture neutrons. At that time graphite was used mainly for the "lead" in pencils, and also in some industries—as a lubricant, for instance. For these purposes it did not need to be nearly as pure as for a pile. Later, after the physicists had built their pile, they calculated that they had used enough graphite to make a pencil for each and every inhabitant of the earth. And this graphite had been of a purity never heard of before.

2

About a year after Fermi and Szilard had decided on the use of graphite to slow down neutrons and to try to produce a chain reaction, a few tons of the materials started to arrive at the physics building at Columbia University. Fermi and his young assistant, Herbert Anderson, who did not mind hard work, became bricklayers and began to stack graphite bricks in one of their laboratories. They made a stocky column of graphite bricks, placed a neutron source under it, observed what happened to the neutrons in the graphite, and gathered data.

The physicists knew that for many months, perhaps for years, they would not have enough pure graphite and uranium to build a large pile and see whether it worked. For the moment this did not matter. Very little was known about the substances with which they were to work, and they were ready to spend much time studying them. After the study of the graphite they undertook the study of uranium. Under what conditions would it undergo fission? How many neutrons would fission free? Would uranium capture some of these neutrons?

As soon as they had a sufficient amount of uranium and graphite, Fermi and his group decided to build a

The Story of Atomic Energy

"small pile." It would not chain react, but it would give information that would later be useful in building a large pile. They took apart their wall of graphite and started again to put down the bricks, this time placing chunks of uranium between layers.

Their work proceeded very slowly. Although they were going to build a "small pile," too small to chain react, it was to be made of several tons of graphite and uranium. The physicists thought they were strong enough to handle so many tons of materials, but they were more used to thinking than to lifting weights. To get the work done more quickly, they hired a dozen of the huskiest boys in the football squad at Columbia University. The results were wonderful. The boys moved packs of fifty or a hundred pounds with the same ease with which the physicists moved five or ten pounds! Soon a black wall went up and reached the ceiling.

The results of research on uranium and graphite and their behavior in a small pile were more and more encouraging. An increasing number of scientists in

Birth of the atomic age

many universities became interested in the achievement of a chain reaction. American and English scientists exchanged views, and their hopes increased. The old dream of unlocking and using the store of energy in the atoms seemed closer and closer to coming true.

President Roosevelt shared the scientists' optimism. He and his advisers decided to speed up atomic research, and they placed top men in charge of different parts of the project. The physicist Arthur H. Compton became the head of all basic research on the chain reaction.

The President's decision to make an all-out effort in the uranium project was announced to the scientists on December 6, 1941. The following day Japanese planes bombed Pearl Harbor. The United States declared war on Japan; Germany and Italy declared war on the United States; and the United States declared war on Germany and Italy. The fear that Germany might make atomic weapons and use them against the Allied nations became more intense. The scientists' race against time became more pressing.

The Story of Atomic Energy

Arthur Compton felt that work would proceed faster if all research under him were done at one university rather than at several. He was a professor at the University of Chicago and considered his university the best suited for atomic research. Besides, Chicago, in the heart of the United States, was out of reach of enemy planes.

Scientists from all over the country began to flock to Chicago. There, work on the chain reaction was top secret. The project was called "Metallurgical Laboratory," or "Met Lab" for short. At a university, this name did not seem strange at all, and it did not reveal what kind of work went on. Scientists at the Met Lab kept to themselves, not mixing much with other members of the faculty. In this way they were less likely to make slips and let secret information leak out.

The Met Lab was well guarded, and no one was allowed to go past the entrance hall—not even the wives of the scientists. If they wanted to talk to their husbands, the husbands had to meet them in the hall.

Husbands did not speak of their work at home. Not until after the end of the war did wives, children, and the other people learn what kind of research had been going on at the Met Lab in wartime.

3

Back at Columbia University, the physicists took apart their small pile. They packed the graphite bricks, chunks of uranium, neutron sources, Geiger counters, and all the other things with which they had been working, and moved to Chicago.

In Chicago they had hoped to find a really big room in which to build a large pile. But the armed forces, which had been taking over large buildings in many cities and towns, had already taken over the largest places around the University of Chicago. The biggest room that the Met Lab could get for its pile was a squash court under the stands of the university stadium. It was 30 feet wide, 60 feet long, and 26 feet high—barely large enough for the pile planned by the Met Lab.

The physicists did not yet have enough uranium and graphite for a large pile, and in the squash court they again built small piles. From the behavior of one of these small piles they learned for the first time that a chain reaction was possible in practice. The uranium and graphite were sufficiently pure; the distribution of uranium chunks in the graphite bricks was good; calculations showed that a large pile would chain react. Yet, the physicists could not build the large pile at once because they lacked materials.

While waiting for more materials, Herbert Anderson went to the Goodyear Rubber Company and placed an order for a six-sided balloon. The Goodyear people had never heard of such a thing. But Anderson insisted, and a couple of months later a huge balloon of rubberized cloth arrived at the Met Lab.

The physicists had calculated that their pile would reach almost to the ceiling of the squash court. But they did not trust their calculations entirely, and they

Birth of the atomic age

were afraid to take chances. They could not push the ceiling up, but they could do something else—they could remove the air around the pile. Then it would not need to be so large, for air captures many neutrons, and they are lost for fission. However, the physicists could not remove the air from the entire court because they had to breathe. What they could do—and what they did—was to build the pile inside a balloon. They could pump the air out of it, if they had to.

The balloon reached from floor to ceiling. Fermi and his group fastened all but one of its six sides, and started to assemble the pile inside it. First, though, they built a frame of wood to support the pile before they began putting graphite bricks and chunks of uranium in place.

In the court, the graphite bricks were being machined to make them fit, and from the machines graphite dust spread everywhere. It made the floor black and slippery. Black figures covered with graphite dust skidded on it. Everything in the squash court became black.

The Story of Atomic Energy

The pile grew until it looked like a huge ball flattened at the top. The physicists found that it was ready to chain react before they had placed the last layers on it. There was no need to pump out the air that surrounded the pile; the balloon had not really been necessary and it remained open, with one side unfastened.

4

On the morning of December 2, 1942, the pile was ready for its final test. Almost four years had gone by since the day Niels Bohr had landed in the United States and brought the news of the discovery of fission. They had been years of hard work, serious study, and great effort. The men who had given their time to that work, study, and effort were now ready to prove that their pile was a success, that fission had unlocked the store of energy in the atoms and thus given a new source of energy to mankind.

About twenty people gathered in the squash court

Birth of the atomic age

on that cold December morning. Among them was a young woman, Leona Wood (now Mrs. John Marshall), who had worked hard and done a man's job; all the others were men.

Three young men climbed to the top of the pile, right under the ceiling. It was a joke among the others that the three were a "suicide squad," sitting in the most dangerous spot. They were like firemen; if something went wrong with the pile and the pile got out of control, they would "put it out" by pouring cadmium on it. (Cadmium is a substance that captures neutrons and stops a chain reaction.)

Another man, George Weil, stood on the floor next to a rod that stuck out from the inside of the pile. All the others climbed onto a balcony to one side of the pile.

Fermi directed the experiment from the balcony, and as he spoke, the others were silent, attentive.

"We shall soon begin our experiment," Fermi said. "The rod that sticks out of the pile is made of cadmium. More than thirteen feet of it are inside the pile. Cadmium captures many, many neutrons, and unless we pull most of the rod out of the pile, the pile cannot chain react. George will pull out the rod a little at a time, as I shall tell him. When the pile starts to chain react, this pen will trace a line that will go up and up."

Fermi pointed to an indicator that could move along a roll of paper. Then he went on:

"We shall take measurements and make sure that the pile will act as we have calculated. Now George will pull out the rod one foot. The Geiger counters here will click faster. Go ahead, George."

As Fermi spoke his gray eyes showed that he was thinking hard. Then he grinned with confidence. George Weil pulled the rod out one foot, and the Geiger counters stepped up their clicking. Fermi made some calculations. The experiment went on step by step, as Fermi checked to see that the pile was working in accordance with his calculations. The morning gave way to noon.

Everybody in the squash court was absorbed in the

Birth of the atomic age

experiment, and only Fermi noticed that time was passing. Suddenly he said, "Let's go to lunch," and thus broke the spell.

After lunch they went back to the squash court where again Fermi assumed command. He took more measurements and instructed Weil to continue pulling out the rod bit by bit. At last he said: "George, pull it out another foot. This will do it. The pile will chain react. This pen will go up and up."

Under the roof of the balloon the "suicide squad" became alert. The men and the woman on the balcony almost stopped breathing. If something were to happen, if Fermi should ever lose control of the chain reaction . . .

They could have spared themselves that moment of suspense, perhaps of fear, for the pile acted just as Fermi had said it would. The counters stepped up, the pen traced a line on the paper, up and up. The chain reaction was achieved and kept under control.

For almost half an hour the pile produced atomic energy. Then Fermi told Weil to push the rod back into the pile, and the chain reaction stopped. The experiment was completed. It spelled success.

Among the physicists in the squash court that day was Eugene Wigner, who, together with Szilard, had persuaded Einstein to write the all-important letter to President Roosevelt. Even before joining the Metallurgical Project, Wigner had begun to study some particular aspects of the chain reaction; he had solved several problems and so had greatly contributed to the success of the pile. He now brought out a bottle of Italian wine in honor of Fermi, and all those present drank it from paper cups. Then they all signed the label on the empty bottle. On that bottle there is the only written list of the men and the woman who witnessed the first chain reaction. One of the young physicists took the bottle to his home, and, so far as is known, he still has it.

Later that same afternoon the director of the Met Lab, Professor Arthur Compton, felt that he should let Professor James Conant know how the experiment had gone. Conant was one of the top men in the or-

Birth of the atomic age

ganization of all scientific research sponsored by the United States government.

Conant was in Cambridge, Massachusetts, and Compton called him on the telephone from Chicago. But Compton could not say, "Fermi has achieved the chain reaction," because anyone who overheard would have learned a great secret.

Instead, Compton announced, "You'll be interested to know that the Italian Navigator has just landed in the new world."

"Is that so!" Conant exclaimed. "Were the natives friendly?"

Compton answered, "Everyone landed safe and happy."

December 2, 1942, marks the birth of the atomic age. Several years later a plaque was placed on the wall near the entrance to the squash court. It read:

> ON DECEMBER 2, 1942
> MAN ACHIEVED HERE
> THE FIRST SELF-SUSTAINING CHAIN REACTION
> AND THEREBY INITIATED THE
> CONTROLLED RELEASE OF NUCLEAR ENERGY

8

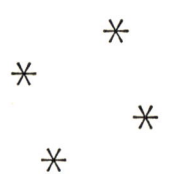

Plans for three secret cities

1

The Chicago pile was a great scientific success; it showed that men could at will make atoms give off their inner energy and that this energy could be kept under control. Because of its success, it ushered in the atomic age. Yet the Chicago pile was only an experiment and did not produce power that could be used. On December 2, 1942, the power developed by the pile was at most sufficient to light the bulb of a small flashlight (half a watt). A few days later the pile was

Plans for three secret cities

operated at a higher power and it might have kept four ordinary bulbs lighted. In the pile, this power built up relatively slowly, not with the violence needed for an explosion. Scientists were still far from making the "extremely powerful bombs" that Einstein had mentioned in his letter to President Roosevelt.

These bombs were what our army wanted, because we were at war and it seemed likely that the fighting side which produced atomic weapons first would have a great advantage over the other. The United States Army was so interested in getting atomic weapons that it had taken charge of the uranium project in the summer of 1942, while Fermi and his group in Chicago were still waiting for materials with which to build their pile. The army had created a special unit to direct the uranium project and had given it the name "Manhattan District." It was a name with no particular meaning, which well hid the secret that the army was interested in atomic research.

Soon General Leslie R. Groves of the U. S. Corps of Engineers became the head of the Manhattan District.

The Story of Atomic Energy

He was a sturdy, heavy-set man who in the past had been concerned mostly with building roads. He knew how to give orders and obtain obedience at once, even when he had to keep secret the reasons for his orders.

General Groves had seen the scientists at work and had great faith in their ability. Even before the first chain reaction was achieved, he had been carrying out plans for the production of atomic bombs. In behalf of our government, he had bought three vast tracts of land in three different states, thousands of miles apart. Within a few months a secret "atomic" city sprang up on each of these tracts. Each city undertook one part of the work on atomic bombs.

To understand the reasons for the three secret cities and their work, we must go back to the time when the news of fission had reached the United States. We must see what other scientists had been doing while Fermi, Szilard, and their assistants were studying the problems of producing a chain reaction.

Plans for three secret cities

2

As we have seen, the discovery of fission showed that when neutrons hit uranium atoms some uranium atoms split into two almost equal chunks and gave off energy. Other uranium atoms did not split. Was it possible to tell which uranium atoms were likely to split into two chunks?

At first the scientists had no answer, but they set themselves to study this question. They knew that natural uranium contains two isotopes: uranium 238 and uranium 235. (The numbers 238 and 235 indicate the atomic mass of the two isotopes.) Soon the scientists found that only uranium 235 is likely to split into two chunks giving off neutrons and energy. When an atom of uranium 238 is hit by a neutron, it captures the neutron but does not split. In the language now used in atomic science, we may say that uranium 235 is *fissionable* and that uranium 238 is not fissionable.

Unfortunately, natural uranium contains about 140

times more uranium 238 than uranium 235. This is one of the reasons why for such a long time scientists did not know whether a chain reaction was at all possible.

Scientists realized that they would never be able to produce an explosion starting with natural uranium, even if they succeeded in achieving a chain reaction in this material. The uranium 238 contained in natural uranium would capture many neutrons, and not enough neutrons would be left to produce an explosive chain reaction.

However, scientists could try to separate the very small amount of uranium 235 from the much larger amount of uranium 238 in natural uranium. They knew this would be extremely difficult. It is usually easy to separate different elements; for instance, the oxygen and hydrogen contained in water, or the chlorine and sodium in salt. Different elements can be separated by chemical methods.

But isotopes are different kinds of the same element, and in all chemical reactions they stay together. In the past, scientists had found ways of separating some isotopes, but the amounts separated had always been extremely small. For an explosion a large amount of uranium 235 would be needed.

Scientists knew that they would have to try several of the known methods of separation. Perhaps they would have to invent new methods, and find out if at least one of them would work for separating large quantities of uranium 235 from uranium 238. They went about their task with great patience and determination. Soon they succeeded in separating tiny amounts of uranium 235.

3

Meanwhile a new discovery pointed the way to another possible material for making bombs. This discovery is of great interest to us, because we may consider it the last word in the riddle of element 93.

The work that led to this discovery began when

The Story of Atomic Energy

scientists learned that uranium 238 is not fissionable. Then, at the University of California in Berkeley, physicists and chemists began to study what happens to uranium 238 when it captures a neutron without undergoing fission. One of the physicists in this group was Emilio Segré, who in Rome had worked with Fermi on the first neutron bombardments. His knowledge of neutrons and uranium atoms was very helpful to the whole group.

As a further help, Ernest Lawrence, the inventor of cyclotrons, had built a very powerful cyclotron in Berkeley. With particles sped up in this cyclotron, the scientists could make more powerful sources of neutrons than those made by Fermi at Columbia University. And Fermi's sources were already 100,000 times more powerful than the neutron "guns" in Rome. Using the Berkeley cyclotron, scientists could now keep uranium under a heavy bombardment and could hit a very large number of uranium atoms. They could more easily recognize what happened when neutrons hit uranium 238.

Plans for three secret cities

Thus the Berkeley scientists discovered that a nucleus of uranium 238, when it captures a neutron, becomes a nucleus of uranium 239. Uranium 239 is radioactive and gives off beta particles. A beta particle carries a negative charge *1*. A nucleus of uranium 239, when it gives off a beta particle, loses a negative charge *1*. This is equivalent to saying that it acquires a positive charge *1*. Its atomic number changes from 92 to 93. The nucleus of uranium 239 transforms into a nucleus of . . . element 93.

This discovery entirely cleared the riddle of element 93. When the physicists in Rome had bombarded uranium with slow neutrons, they had produced fission in uranium 235; they had also made at least a few atoms of element 93. But they had not been able to understand what they had done.

Later Hahn, Meitner, and Strassmann had come very close to discovering the true element 93. Uranium 239, from which element 93 is formed, has a half life of twenty-three minutes. When the Berlin scientists had repeated Fermi's experiments, they had found a

The Story of Atomic Energy

substance with that same half life. They had also recognized that it was an isotope of uranium and that it emitted beta particles. Because of these facts, the Berlin team knew that their substance would change into an isotope of element 93. They looked for this isotope, but could not detect it, for their materials were too weak.

Element 93 is now called neptunium. It decays fast and changes into element 94, plutonium. *Plutonium is fissionable:* when it is hit by neutrons, some of its atoms split in two and give off energy and neutrons. Plutonium decays very slowly; its half life is 24,000 years.

The scientists at the University of California realized that plutonium would be a good material for atomic bombs; if they could obtain several pounds of it they could hope to make it explode. But after working about a year to make some of it, they had an amount of plutonium metal only as big as a grain of table salt.

Not even with the most powerful cyclotrons would

Plans for three secret cities

the scientists be able to make enough plutonium in time to help win the war. Piles would give quicker results; in a pile some of the neutrons that come from fission would hit uranium 235, produce further fission and a chain reaction. Other neutrons would hit uranium 238, and change it first into neptunium, and then into plutonium. This plutonium could be taken out of the pile and used for weapons.

But at the time when the California scientists were making plutonium with the cyclotron, the physicists at Columbia University had not yet moved to Chicago and had not started construction of the first chain-reacting pile. The scientists interested in the production of plutonium went on studying its properties and behavior; to do this, they had only the very tiny amounts that could be made with cyclotrons.

4

We have now a full picture of the state of atomic research at the time when the army took over the uranium project, and General Groves began making plans for the production of atomic weapons. The Chicago pile was under construction, and physicists had not yet proved that they could achieve a chain reaction. Plutonium was being made in exceedingly small amounts. Unless piles worked well, there was no hope of making it in quantities sufficient for an explosion, in time to help win the war. Uranium 235 was being separated in very tiny amounts, much smaller than those needed for an explosion.

Looking backward to that time, we may think that atomic weapons were then a dream of the scientists. Yet they did not seem a dream to those who had seen the scientists at work, or who had checked the precision of the scientists' predictions. On the basis of these predictions several American industries agreed to help the uranium project by separating uranium 235 and producing plutonium on an industrial scale. General Groves began looking for places suited for secret cities.

9

The city that made uranium 235

1

Places for secret cities must fill certain requirements. They must be far from cities, towns, and highways; otherwise too many people can see them. They must spread over considerable stretches of ground and yet be concealed as much as possible.

Luckily, the United States is a vast country; parts of it are still wild and sparsely populated, and land for secret cities was not hard to find.

The first purchase was made in the fall of 1942

The Story of Atomic Energy

when the Manhattan District bought a tract in the Tennessee Valley, along the Clinch River. It was pleasant country, with low hills and sunny valleys covered with green pastures and woods. Quiet rivers and streams followed the soft curves of the valleys. In this kind of land it was easy to hide buildings, either at the bottom of valleys or in the folds between the hills. The rivers carried enough water for a city and for large factories.

Among the scientists in the uranium project this tract of land became known as "Site X." There the secret city of Oak Ridge grew as fast as a mushroom.

Homes went up by the hundreds. Along with them went the facilities that hundreds of families need: schools, churches, stores, theaters, and eating places. There was no time to pave streets or sidewalks. When the weather was dry, the hills and valleys became covered with dense clouds of dust, and when it rained, there were seas of mud. Feet sank deep into the mud, and shoes and trousers became coated with a thick, stiff layer of clay.

The city that made uranium 235

Near the city, industrial plants went up. They were called "Clinton Engineering Works," another name which, like "Manhattan District" or "Metallurgic Laboratory," did not give away secrets. The main task of the Clinton Engineering Works was the separation of uranium 235 from uranium 238.

One plant was to achieve this separation by a method called *gaseous diffusion*. The idea is simple. Natural uranium, which is commonly a metal, can combine with fluorine and form a gas. In the process of gaseous diffusion, this uranium gas is forced through special filters which let lighter gases pass through or, as the physicists say, diffuse, a little faster than heavier gases. The uranium gas containing uranium 235 is a little lighter and goes through the filter a little faster than the uranium gas containing uranium 238.

The passage through the filter is stopped when only part of the gas has gone through. This part is a little richer in uranium 235 than the part left behind. If the richer part is forced through another filter, part of it becomes even richer in uranium 235. Passage through

The Story of Atomic Energy

a single filter enriches the uranium gas very little, and, to obtain practical results, the gas must be forced through thousands of filters. Thousands of pumps are needed, and the gas must travel through thousands of miles of pipes.

The gaseous diffusion plant at Oak Ridge was to become one of the largest industrial plants ever built. It was to use as much electricity as the city of New York.

2

Another plant of the Clinton Engineering Works separated uranium 235 by using a huge magnet. We have already seen that a magnet can bend the path of charged particles; the path of lighter particles will be bent more than the path of heavier particles. A big magnet will also bend the molecules of a uranium salt that has been vaporized and whose molecules have been charged. Because the molecules containing uranium 235 are lighter than those containing uranium 238, their path is bent more. In this way, the molecules containing uranium 235 become separated from those containing uranium 238.

At the time the Clinton Engineering Works were built, the biggest magnets existing were those of the most powerful cyclotrons. Even so, they were not big enough. The amounts of uranium 235 separated by them were too small, and too much time would be needed to produce enough of it for weapons. But a lucky circumstance helped the scientists.

Before the war Ernest Lawrence had started building a *giant* cyclotron, bigger and more powerful than any existing at that time. At the beginning of the war its construction had been halted, for a giant cyclotron had not seemed essential for the war effort. But the magnet planned for the cyclotron was almost ready, and now it was quickly finished, for Lawrence realized that it could be used to separate uranium 235.

It was a huge magnet weighing 4900 tons and shaped like an oval ring. The men at Oak Ridge dug an immense hole and put the magnet in it. Ernest Lawrence, who supervised the work, called the magnet "the race track." It really looked like a track for some important race; as indeed it was, for it produced uranium 235 fast and helped the scientists in their race with time.

Large magnets are made of a steel core, around which electric coils are wound. When an electric current is sent into the coils, the steel core becomes a magnet.

When Lawrence's giant magnet was brought to Oak Ridge, it did not yet have coils. A very great quantity of copper would have been required to make coils for such a big magnet; but copper was very scarce at that time because the Army needed all it could get. Coils could be made of silver, but it was frightfully expensive.

In the end, the United States Treasury agreed to lend the silver from its reserve. An army colonel went to make arrangements with the Assistant Secretary of the Treasury.

The city that made uranium 235

"How much silver do you need?" asked the Assistant Secretary.

"About fifteen thousand tons," the colonel replied.

The other jumped in his chair. "Young man," he said, "when we talk of silver here, we speak in terms of ounces!"

Despite this sharp reply, the colonel got the amount he wanted. It served its purpose and was returned after the end of the war.

10

The city that made plutonium

1

The largest of the three tracts of land that General Groves bought was in the State of Washington along the Columbia River, north of the city of Pasco. Most of the land was barren; vast, sandy stretches of gray plains and hills were covered here and there with carpets of gray sagebrush. Only where men had irrigated the soil with water pumped from the Columbia River did patches of green farmland break the grayness of the landscape. Few people lived there, and the wild

The city that made plutonium

animals were not often disturbed. There were only two small villages, Hanford and Richland, each with a population of about 250 inhabitants.

It was an ideal site for a secret city. On the advice of scientists and men from industry, General Groves chose this site for the city and the big piles that were to produce plutonium. In time, the village of Richland was to grow into a large, well-built city for the people who operated the piles and for their families.

While Richland was being planned and built, construction workers lived at Hanford in a camp of huts, barracks, and trailers. This camp grew so fast that within a year it housed some 60,000 people and became the fourth largest city in the State of Washington.

In Hanford there were eight immense mess halls where workers were served the best meals that could be had in wartime. In the halls hung signs that gave such advice as, "Don't talk shop" and "Don't discuss your job." The signs reminded the men that they were doing secret work, and that no one was to know what another's job was. The men ate in silence, and the halls were so quiet that it seemed hard to believe that thousands of men were eating. The crowds of diners were so large that fifty to sixty tons of food were served at each meal.

At night the men made up for having been quiet while eating; there were all sorts of places where they could have fun. Especially popular was a huge auditorium that could hold four thousand dancers. It had been built in only ten days, for in Hanford everything went up fast.

As Richland grew, and the construction of piles was completed, there was no longer need for the Hanford camp. It was abandoned, and Hanford became a ghost town. Its name remained; the piles and the plants that went with them were called "Hanford Engineering Works."

2

The piles at Hanford were similar to the Chicago pile, but they were much larger. Fermi and his group in Chicago had thought that their pile was big, for it filled a room almost as large as a church. Yet it was small by other standards; calculations showed that the Chicago pile would have had to be kept going at least 70,000 years in order to produce enough plutonium for one bomb. The Hanford piles, on the other hand, were really big. Once completed, they towered in the barren countryside like structures built by giants.

Constructing huge piles had raised many problems. As we know, the Chicago pile was built to show that a chain reaction was possible; it was not built to produce energy or plutonium. Operated at a low power, it did not produce much heat and radioactivity. But the Hanford piles were operated at a high power and gave off a great deal of energy and strong radiation.

The Story of Atomic Energy

Because radiation is very dangerous to men, animals, and plants, big piles must be enclosed in thick walls of concrete, steel, or other material that stops all radiation. These protective walls are called the *shielding* of a pile.

To start, regulate, and stop the first chain reaction in the Chicago pile, George Weil had pulled out or pushed in a cadmium rod by hand. The many rods that control the chain reaction in a big pile are operated by remote control from outside the shielding.

Because big piles produce much heat, they must be cooled. (All devices producing heat are cooled. If the air fan in a car fails to work, parts of the engine may melt and the car may be wrecked.) Water is a good *coolant*. The Columbia River, one of the largest in the United States, could supply all the water needed—this was one of the reasons why General Groves had chosen the land along the Columbia River for the three big piles.

Huge pumps were built to bring water from the

The city that made plutonium

river. The water was to circulate inside the piles, cool them, and then be dumped back into the Columbia River. The engineers who planned the pumps and the rerouting of the water had to worry about something that may seem unimportant: the safety of the fish. The Columbia River is a rich source of fish and is famous for its Chinook salmon, white sturgeon, and smelt. The fish industry, one of the main resources of the State of Washington, had to be protected at all costs.

The fish in the river faced a double danger: pumps and radioactivity. The pumps could suck the fish up and crush them. To keep them away from the pumps, the Hanford engineers built fish ladders and placed screens in front of all water intakes. Then water could be pumped from the river without danger to the fish. But they still had to be protected from radioactivity, for after the water had circulated inside the piles, it carried along some of the radioactivity that piles produce. Although this was not strong, there was enough

The Story of Atomic Energy

to hurt the fish if the water were sent directly back into the river. To avoid this, the water was stored in artificial ponds or lakes until its radioactivity decayed.

3

While the Hanford piles were chain reacting, some uranium 238 changed into plutonium. After a while the plutonium had to be separated from the uranium in which it formed. In principle the separation is easy, since uranium and plutonium are different elements, and it is possible to separate them by chemical methods. In practice the separation is not so easy. Uranium in which plutonium has formed contains many products of fission, some of which are strongly radioactive and extremely dangerous. Unless handled with special precautions, they seriously injure workers, or even cause death.

At Hanford the uranium containing plutonium was removed from the piles by remote control and dumped

The city that made plutonium

into a deep basin filled with water. Water, an excellent shielding, absorbed all the radiation, so that none of it could escape into the air. The uranium was then dragged under water through deep artificial canyons. It was thus brought to separation plants, larger than football fields, where it was chemically treated by remote control.

In planning the piles and the separation plants, the engineers always kept in mind the possibility of accidents that might allow radiation to escape into the air. To reduce this danger, they built the separation plants at great distances from the piles. For the convenience of workers, a small railroad connected each pile to its separation plant.

The tract of land that the Manhattan District had first bought, large as it was, soon proved too small. As the Hanford Engineering Works grew and expanded, the Manhattan District acquired more land. Before the end of the war, the project along the Columbia River spread over an area almost as large as the State of Rhode Island. On this area ran 350 miles of newly built highways, and 44 railroad locomotives pulled trains on 160 miles of tracks.

4

While solving the problems of producing plutonium, many scientists, engineers, and men from industry had to improve their knowledge of nuclear physics. Because this was still a very young science, there was only one really good book on the subject. Soon thousands of orders for the volume were flowing from the Hanford Engineering Works, and the publishers began to wonder what was going on in this unheard-of place.

To satisfy their curiosity, they sent a man to find out why a village, marked on the maps as having 250 people, should want so many copies of their book. The man was given a cool reception—and no information. Neither he nor any other outsider was to know that in the desert country along the Columbia River, the army

The city that made plutonium
and scientists were working together on an atomic project.

After this incident, the Hanford address disappeared from orders for the book, and the scientists had to obtain it by roundabout means.

11

✶
 ✶
  ✶
   ✶
  ✶

The most secret of the secret cities

1

General Groves felt that the study of all problems related to the design and construction of atomic bombs should be carried out in an even more isolated spot than those for the production of plutonium and of uranium 235. He found an ideal place.

On a lonely mesa along the Los Alamos Canyon in New Mexico, at 7200 feet above sea level, there was a small school for boys. It had perhaps a dozen stone or log cabins where the teachers lived, and a few other

The most secret of the secret cities

buildings for classes and pupils' living quarters. A soft arc of green hills, the Jemez range, surrounded the mesa to the west. To the east the flat top of the mesa ended suddenly. Far below, the vast desert began and stretched for miles and miles—a waste of sand, cacti, and a few piñon trees. A thin, winding strip of green land cut through the desert, marking the path of the Rio Grande River. Along the green fertile strip were ancient Indian pueblos and Spanish-American villages.

A narrow mountain road connected the school on the mesa with the highway down in the valley of the Rio Grande. The nearest town, Santa Fe, was forty miles away, and it was over sixty miles to the nearest railroad. The Los Alamos school was indeed secluded!

The school principal must have been surprised when an army officer and an intellectual-looking young man called to see him and explained that the army wished to buy the school for secret work. The heavy-set army officer talking in authoritative tones was General Groves. The younger man, with rounded shoulders and narrow intelligent eyes, chewed steadily on a pipe and seemed to act as a guide to the general. He was J. Robert Oppenheimer, a physicist to whom New Mexico was almost home, for his family owned a ranch in the New Mexican mountains and spent much time there.

In November 1942 the Manhattan District bought the school, and soon army engineers began building homes and laboratories around it. In constructing the laboratories, they followed the vague directives of scientists who could not explain what kind of work was to be done. As the engineers finished a group of buildings, the scientists asked for more. And so the most secret of the three secret cities began to grow.

Scientists from all parts of the United States and from England went to live in that city and disappeared from the world. For two and a half years that city was not marked on the maps, was not part of New Mexico, and its residents could not vote. To the rest of the world it did not exist at all. It was known as Los Alamos to the people who went to live in it; as Post Office Box 1663, Santa Fe, to their friends and

The most secret of the secret cities

relatives; as "Site Y" to other workers in the uranium project.

All buildings in Los Alamos were painted green and from a distance it was hard to distinguish them from the green grass and trees on the mesa. At night there were no lights in the streets. The secret city would not easily be found by enemy planes.

A barbed-wire fence ran around Los Alamos to keep outsiders out and residents in. But most children knew the holes in the fence and sometimes guided their parents through them. Outside the first fence, there was a second one, but, so far as we know, there were no holes in it. The city had two gates. The West Gate led toward the Jemez hills. From the East Gate a winding road went from the top of the mesa straight down into the desert and the Rio Grande valley. Both gates were heavily guarded, and no one, not even a young child, could enter or leave Los Alamos without showing his pass to the guards. It was a favorite game among the children to lie low on the bottom of a car

The Story of Atomic Energy

going through a gate, and try to be smuggled in without showing their pass.

Security Officers read all mail to make sure that people in Los Alamos did not write about secret matters. Once a physicist fond of practical jokes began writing letters in a code and sent the key to the Security Officers. It is said that another time the same physicist wrote in Chinese characters. Soon the Security Office announced that Los Alamos residents were to write letters only in such common languages as English, Spanish, French, and Italian. Codes were clearly not welcome!

The army ran the city in military fashion, to the sound of sirens. The day started at 7:00 A.M. when the first siren went off. An hour later, when the second siren blew, it was time to start work. Men and women stopped at the gate of the Technical Area, where the secret work went on, and showed their badges to the guards. Scientists wore white badges; other employes blue badges. A blue badge indicated that the person who wore it should not be told anything that was top

The most secret of the secret cities

secret. At noon the sirens announced lunch hour, later the return to work and, finally, the end of the working day.

2

By late summer of 1944 many top scientists from the United States and other countries were living in this extremely well-guarded and well-regulated city. After the war was over, Professor H. D. Smyth wrote, in an official report on the wartime development of atomic science: ". . . the end of 1944 found an extraordinary galaxy of scientific stars gathered on this New Mexican mesa."

According to a story that circulated widely in Los Alamos, General Groves used quite different words to say the same thing. At about the end of 1944 he gathered his officers and told them (so the story goes): "At great expense we have gathered on this mesa the largest collection of crackpots ever seen." General

The Story of Atomic Energy

Groves was fond of his "crackpots," the scientists, and wanted his officers to take good care of them.

These "crackpots"—or scientific "stars"—many of whom spoke with a thick foreign accent, and all of whom seemed steadily immersed in deep thoughts, included several scientists already mentioned. Among them were Enrico Fermi, Emilio Segré, Herbert Anderson, and Robert Oppenheimer. J. Robert Oppenheimer, or Oppie, as his friends called him, was the director of research in Los Alamos and the soul of the project. He went around the Technical Area with his pipe in his mouth, and in his quiet way asked questions without seeming to ask, kept informed about all work, and was in close touch with everyone. His enthusiasm and zeal spurred others to do their best, and most of the success of the project is due to him.

Both Fermi and Oppie had arrived in Los Alamos accompanied by their bodyguards. Shortly after General Groves had taken charge of the Manhattan District, and long before he recommended the "crackpots"

The most secret of the secret cities

to the care of his army officers on the mesa, he had assigned a bodyguard to each of some half-dozen top scientists. This was one of the many measures he had taken to protect the leading physicists on the uranium project. Outside Los Alamos, bodyguards always accompanied their charges, being especially careful not to let them travel alone or walk by themselves at night. In Los Alamos, a well-guarded city, Fermi and Oppie went around without bodyguards; but when they took trips to other places, the bodyguards followed them.

One of the best-known characters on the mesa was "Mr. Nicholas Baker." He was a heavy-set man with a big, gray-haired head and stooping shoulders who always looked preoccupied. When he walked about town he did not seem to see where he was going, and when he talked, only a whisper came from his mouth. He was a little older than the other scientists, and all looked upon him with respect and awe.

Those who had known him in the past called him "Uncle Nick," for they found it hard to say "Mr.

Baker." And they could not call him by his true name, Niels Bohr. It was a top secret that the most famous atomic physicist in the world was in Los Alamos.

When Emilio Segré, Fermi's old friend, arrived in Los Alamos, he was an "enemy alien." The United States and Italy were at war with one another, and Segré was still an Italian citizen; it takes five years of residence in the United States for a foreigner to become an American citizen. The fact that Los Alamos was a secret city made matters difficult, for not even the judge in charge of awarding United States citizenship knew that a place called Los Alamos existed.

At last a day was set for Segré to become naturalized. Segré and his witnesses (who were to say he would make a good citizen) appeared in the Federal Court of Santa Fe. Segré was duly sworn and received his citizenship papers from the judge. But a few days later the judge informed Segré that these papers were not valid. The law provided that no citizenship papers could be issued within 60 days before an election; there was going to be an election in New Mexico, and

The most secret of the secret cities

Segré had been late by one day. He had to start all over again.

The American Oppie, the Italians Fermi and Segré, the Danish Bohr, are but a few examples of the many nationalities represented in Los Alamos. One group, known as the "British Mission," greatly added to the variety of the crackpots' national traits. The United States, Great Britain, and Canada were allies in the war, and they had decided to work together and to establish all their atomic projects in North America. One result of this decision was the arrival in Los Alamos of a group of scientists from England. The head of this mission was James Chadwick, discoverer of the neutron.

The scientists of the British mission were not all English born. They included men from Switzerland, Germany, Austria, and Poland. One of them was Otto Frisch, the physicist who, with Lise Meitner, had interpreted fission and measured the energy that it releases. He became well known in Los Alamos, both as an excellent piano player and as a poor driver. Once, his car skidded on a freshly graveled road and ran into a tree; as a result he ended in the Los Alamos hospital.

At the end of the war the members of the British mission left Los Alamos, but first they gave a huge party for their American friends (including those with strong foreign accents). It is said that the British wives cooked for weeks, only to see the mountains of food they had prepared disappear in an hour when they served their guests.

3

Each of the three secret cities did its own part of the work. Oak Ridge separated uranium 235, both in the gaseous diffusion plant and with the giant magnet. Hanford operated the three big piles and produced plutonium. Los Alamos solved the problems of making an explosion and building bombs.

On a night in July, 1945, at "Trinity," the first

The most secret of the secret cities

atomic explosion went off. "Trinity" was a code name for Alamogordo, a place in the New Mexico desert almost two hundred miles south of Los Alamos. The explosion at Trinity was a test, meant to show whether atomic bombs would work according to calculations. It proved more powerful than the scientists had anticipated, and produced a flash of light so brilliant that it was seen by a blind girl many miles away. In distant Los Alamos, a man who could not sleep noticed a strange light.

Later General Farrell described the explosion in a report to the War Department: "The whole country was lighted by a searching light with the intensity many times that of the midday sun. It was golden, purple, violet, gray, and blue. It lighted every peak, crevasse, and ridge of the near-by mountain range with a clarity and beauty that cannot be described. . . . Thirty seconds after the explosion came first the air blast, pressing hard against the people and things; to be followed almost immediately by the strong, sus-

The Story of Atomic Energy

tained, awesome roar which warned of doomsday. . . ." A big cloud shaped like a huge mushroom went up in the air.

The explosion dug a crater in the desert half a mile in diameter and melted the sand on the surface of this crater. When the sand hardened again, it lined the crater with a sheet of green glass.

The test at Trinity was soon followed by the actual use of atomic bombs in the war. It was early August, 1945, and Germany had already surrendered. President Roosevelt had died the previous April, and President Truman had taken his place. Truman and the American nation wanted a speedy victory. The first atomic bomb was dropped on the city of Hiroshima in Japan, and a few days later a second bomb exploded on Nagasaki. After the second bomb Japan surrendered, and the Second World War came to an end. The United States and its allies were the victors on all fronts.

From Oak Ridge, Hanford, and Los Alamos, many scientists went back to teach and to do research in the universities. When our country had been in danger, they had willingly accepted secrecy and work that led to weapons, but in peacetime they did not want to make weapons or to work in secrecy. They preferred fields of research in which they were entirely free to discuss ideas and achievements.

12

Atoms for peace

1

The end of the Second World War did not stop research on atomic energy. On the contrary, atomic studies received a new impetus. Many scientists turned their attention from atomic weapons to the peaceful uses of atomic energy. They tried to find ways by which atomic energy could bring benefits to mankind. Atomic work spread from Oak Ridge, Hanford, and Los Alamos to other atomic centers, to universities, hospitals, and industries.

Atoms for peace

Large atomic projects were set up in other countries: in England and Canada, which had helped the United States develop atomic weapons during the war; in the Soviet Union; and in France. A few other European countries took up atomic research on a smaller scale.

For many years the work of atomic scientists everywhere remained in large part secret. It is not possible to separate entirely the peaceful from the military uses of atomic energy, and no country wanted to give away information that might help other countries to build weapons.

The fact is that, although the war had ended, the world was not at peace. A period known as the "cold war" set in. The democratic Western countries and the communist Eastern countries formed two large blocs, each with different ideas about freedom and the rights of men. The Eastern bloc was governed by dictators. These dictators enclosed their countries in a kind of imaginary curtain, the Iron Curtain, which did not permit men or information to pass through.

The Story of Atomic Energy

The two blocs were extremely suspicious of each other's intentions. Each side was afraid that the other would turn the cold war into a true war and start an attack with atomic weapons of great destructiveness. Both sides felt that they should be ready to defend themselves in case of an attack.

The countries that knew how to build atomic weapons went on building them. Several years went by. President Eisenhower succeeded President Truman.

In December, 1953, Eisenhower made a bold proposal before the General Assembly of the United Nations. The President knew that the countries with large atomic projects were using most of their uranium and other fissionable materials to make atomic weapons. He proposed that each of these countries begin to pool some of its fissionable materials and distribute them to other countries for peaceful uses. He was sure that in the hands of scientists and engineers these materials would help scientific research, medicine, and agriculture, and would produce abundant electricity in the power-starved countries of the world.

Atoms for peace

President Eisenhower concluded his address with a promise to the United Nations: ". . . the United States pledges before you—and therefore before the world—its determination . . . to find ways by which the miraculous inventiveness of man shall not be dedicated to his death, but consecrated to his life."

President Eisenhower's address startled many people. A great part of the atomic work had been carried out in secrecy, and the rest had not received great publicity. Few among the general public realized that the energy from atoms could be put to important peacetime use. The majority of people had heard of atomic energy and most people still believed that it could bring only explosions and destruction.

They did not know, as we know now, that atomic energy can be transformed into useful power: electric power to light our cities and keep our industries going; heat for our homes; power to propel our boats; and perhaps, in a not-too-distant future, power to drive train engines, to fly airplanes and rocket ships. Although radioisotopes were already being used, few

The Story of Atomic Energy

people who were not scientists were aware that radioisotopes are produced in very large amounts in piles, along with atomic energy.

Many people did not know about the piles—which are now often called *reactors* because they are no longer made by "piling up" uranium and graphite. It was not general knowledge that the radioisotopes made in reactors have very wide and varied applications: doctors use them to treat diseases, and biologists use them to study the life processes of men, animals, and plants. With their help farmers get better fertilizers, breed species of plants more resistant to disease, produce seeds that yield more plentiful crops, and improve the breeds and products of farm animals.

Nor did many people know that radioisotopes made in reactors are very useful in industry. They are now used, for instance, to test how fast tires, or engine parts, wear out; to gauge the thickness of metal and paper sheets; to detect leaks in oil wells and pipes. Perhaps in the near future their radiations will be used

Atoms for peace

to sterilize food, which will then keep longer, in some cases even without canning or refrigeration.

When, in December, 1953, President Eisenhower spoke before the General Assembly of the United Nations, he was telling the world that atoms can do much good for mankind. His proposal became known as the "Atoms-for-Peace Plan."

If some fissionable materials were used for peaceful ends, as the plan suggested, less would be left for making weapons. As a result, fewer weapons would be built. At the same time, the whole world would benefit from atomic energy. Atomic energy might then bring well-being to poor countries and lessen the tensions in the world.

2

The Atoms-for-Peace Plan had important results. The United States stepped up its program of shipping fissionable materials for atomic research to countries in which they were not produced. It also gave information and technical assistance on their use. Many foreign scientists and engineers came to the United States to learn atomic science and to prepare to teach it to other scientists in their own countries.

At the suggestion of the United States, the United Nations called the first International Conference on the Peaceful Uses of Atomic Energy. This took place in Geneva, Switzerland, in the summer of 1955, and its success surpassed all expectations. Fourteen hundred scientists and government representatives participated in this conference. They came from 73 countries of both the Western and Eastern blocs. For the first time in many, many years the East lifted the Iron Curtain to permit large numbers of its scientists to attend the conference. In Geneva, scientists from the East and from the West experienced great pleasure in getting together. It was as if they had a huge family reunion after a long period of separation due to reasons over which they had no control.

Atoms for peace

Many of the scientists already mentioned in this story were in Geneva at that conference. Niels Bohr was there. He was by then a bit heavier than he had been at Los Alamos, and he stooped a little more when he walked, as if his head, larger than average, had become too big a load for his shoulders. Everyone looked at him with great respect, for he was still the greatest of living atomic scientists. He spoke as softly and unclearly as ever.

One evening Bohr was to give a talk in English. Like all talks at the conference, it was to be translated into three other languages. Through earphones the audience could listen either to Bohr's English lecture or to one of the three translations. The English-speaking scientists were afraid they would understand little of Bohr's talk; his soft mumbling and his strong Danish accent were as famous as Bohr himself. They were startled when through their earphones came words that were perfectly pronounced. The organizers of the conference, knowing of Bohr's speech difficulty, had arranged for an English translation of his English!

The Story of Atomic Energy

Otto Hahn was also in Geneva. He was small and quiet, with a retiring manner. Little tufts of thin, white hair framed his face, and there was often a bewildered expression in his blue eyes, as if he were still astonished at the great things that had come from his discovery of fission.

Ernest Lawrence, the inventor of the cyclotron, met the Russian cyclotron expert, Vladimir Veksler, in Geneva. The two men were very different. Veksler was of slight build, and the little hair he still had was black and sleek. He talked in a very polite, courteous way that seemed a bit old-fashioned by American standards. Compared with him, Lawrence, who was tall, blond, and lively, with the easy manners of a Californian, seemed an overgrown schoolboy. The two men enjoyed meeting each other and talked about cyclotrons whenever they were together.

Veksler and Lawrence were not exceptions. At the Geneva Conference, scientists from the Western and Eastern countries spent much time "talking shop," and they enjoyed it. Their friendly discussions proved to one another their sincere wish to put atomic energy to work for the benefit of mankind.

The Geneva Conference was a great step toward making this wish come true. The countries with atomic knowledge disclosed much information that until then had been kept secret. The less advanced countries learned what atoms can do, and how they can make atoms work for their benefit.

A second conference on the peaceful uses of atomic energy took place in 1958, also in Geneva. American scientists have been at international meetings in Russia, and Russian scientists have visited the United States. The effects of this new spirit are beginning to show, and mankind is reaping the first fruits of the peacetime use of atomic energy.

13

Power from the atoms

1

Among the peaceful uses of atomic energy, perhaps the most important for its practical value is the production of power. At the present time most of the power we need is generated by burning coal and oil. We get these fossil fuels from deposits that were formed some 250 million years ago, under special weather conditions which have not occurred again on earth. When we mine coal or exploit oil wells, we use up reserves that will not be replenished.

At some future time all the coal and oil in the world

Power from the atoms

will be used up, and this time may come sooner than we think; the demand for power is growing at an amazing speed, and to satisfy it we must burn more and more fuel. There are several reasons for the increase in the demand for power: the population of the world is growing very rapidly; many countries that were underdeveloped are now becoming industrialized; and standards of living are rising everywhere. As a result, more and more people consume more and more power in their homes, and they also want more and more goods made with machines that need power to run. The experts say that if the demand for power keeps growing at the present rate, the world reserves of coal and oil will last a few centuries, possibly only one hundred years.

It is fortunate that at this critical moment in human history, man has learned to generate power from atomic energy. Already several atomic plants are producing electricity; two atomic boats have been built; and atomic power is used experimentally to heat homes.

The Story of Atomic Energy

Electric power is generated from atomic energy in atomic power plants. In principle, an atomic plant is not very different from a regular plant generating electricity from fossil fuels. A regular plant consists essentially of a boiler, a turbine, and a generator. In the boiler, coal or oil burns to develop heat which changes water into steam. The steam makes the turbine turn, and the turbine drives the generator. While running, the generator produces electricity, which is then sent into power lines and distributed where needed.

In an atomic power plant, a reactor—a modern atomic pile—takes the place of the boiler. When the reactor chain reacts and releases atomic energy, it becomes very hot. The heat thus produced changes water into steam. As in a regular power plant, the steam turns the turbine, and the turbine drives the generator. The generator produces electricity. So we may consider a reactor as a boiler that "burns" uranium or other fissionable materials. For this reason fissionable materials are now commonly called *nuclear fuels*.

The most modern power plants now being built are

Power from the atoms

entirely enclosed in round domes of steel or other materials that stop the passage of all radioactivity. These domes are meant to protect the population in case a reactor should not work properly and should let radioactivity leak out. In the future, the landscape all over the world may be marked by these round domes. Perhaps our children and grandchildren will consider them to be symbols of the atomic age, as we consider the tall smokestacks of our factories to be symbols of industrial progress.

Atomic power plants are still very expensive, as are all new things. When cars were first built, only rich people could afford them. Likewise, only rich countries can now afford large atomic plants. Yet many countries are constructing smaller plants in which their scientists and engineers can learn how to generate electricity from atoms and how to solve the difficulties that arise when reactors work to make atoms split.

2

The first atomic plant in the world to generate electricity steadily and to send it out over power lines was built in the Soviet Union. It started working in June, 1954. The next year, at the first conference on the peaceful uses of atomic energy, the Russians showed models and a beautiful color film of this plant.

As seen in the movie, the reactor was large and bulky. The nuclear fuel that "burned" in it was slightly enriched uranium. It was not scattered in chunks, as in the first pile built in Chicago, but was made into *fuel elements*. These are nuclear fuel which has been fashioned into long rods, plates, or tubes, and they are easily pulled out when needed. Fuel elements have been used in many reactors built after the Chicago pile.

The Russian reactor contained 128 fuel elements. After it had worked for some time, the fuel elements were *spent:* many uranium atoms had split and many

Power from the atoms

fission products had formed. These products absorbed many neutrons, and not enough neutrons were left to keep the chain reaction going. The spent elements were then pulled out by a huge crane and replaced by fresh ones. Men in white coats and caps operated the crane by remote control.

The Russian atomic plant generated 5,000 kilowatts of electricity. The movie showed how this electricity reached the consumers, and how it was used. It showed, for instance, cows being milked by atomic power on a Russian farm.

The second power plant that went into operation was built at Calder Hall, in England. In October, 1956, Queen Elizabeth II officially inaugurated it. She pulled a switch, and the electricity from the Calder Hall plant began flowing into the power lines. This plant generated ten times as much electric power as the first Russian plant.

In our country we did not build an atomic power plant of industrial size as early as England did, for there was a difference between the needs of the two

The Story of Atomic Energy

countries. England expected a shortage of coal and oil in the near future and wanted to have another source of power as soon as possible. English scientists went ahead and built an atomic power plant with a type of reactor which they knew would work, because it had already been tried. (It was very similar to one of the atomic piles built in the United States during the war.)

The United States had larger reserves of coal and oil, and more money than England. Because we had more coal and oil, we did not need a new source of power as soon as England. Because we had more money, our scientists could plan and build reactors of different types to see which would work better and cost less. In this country, many reactors of small size were constructed with different materials, different nuclear fuels, different substances for slowing down neutrons and for carrying away the heat from fission.

Our scientists found that there was no "best" type of reactor, but that several seemed promising. Our government and industries chose the most promising types, and then embarked on the construction of sev-

Power from the atoms

eral atomic power plants. The first to be completed was the plant at Shippingport, near Pittsburgh, Pennsylvania. In the Shippingport reactor, the substance that slows down neutrons is water. Water was not used in the first atomic pile, because it captures more neutrons than graphite, but the Shippingport reactor makes up for the loss of neutrons in other ways; its fuel, for instance, is enriched uranium which is more fissionable and absorbs fewer neutrons than natural uranium. In this plant, the water that slows down neutrons also cools the reactor.

The Shippingport plant generates 60,000 kilowatts of electricity. It began working in May, 1958, when President Eisenhower sent an electronic impulse to Shippingport from the White House in Washington. The impulse opened a valve and started the electricity flowing through the power lines to the Pittsburgh area.

A much larger plant was built at Dresden, Illinois, 50 miles southwest of Chicago. It went into operation in August, 1960, three and a half years after construction began, and it generates 180,000 kilowatts of electricity. A 190-foot steel sphere houses a *boiling water* reactor, in which the water that slows down neutrons and is heated by the energy released in fission is allowed to boil and directly produce the steam that runs the turbine. Other large plants are under construction in the United States.

Other countries are now building or planning to build atomic power plants, and more countries will do the same as soon as they have trained their scientists and engineers in atomic science. The prospects for an atomic industry developing fast the world over are very good. Yet plans must be continuously revised to fit changing needs. Thus in England the price of oil and coal and the demand for power have not gone up as fast as it was thought they would, and in the summer of 1960 the British government announced that it was slowing down the pace of its atomic program.

In time, atomic power will help underdeveloped countries. In these countries there are large areas without railways or good roads, where it would be difficult to transport coal or oil. But nuclear fuels are much

Power from the atoms

more compact than coal or oil; for one pound of uranium can do the work of more than one million pounds of coal. It may be possible to ship or fly enough uranium to run a reactor in places to which it would not be possible to transport enough coal or oil for a regular power plant.

The best type of reactor for distant areas may be a small "package" reactor which can be transported by air. When "package" reactors, which are now under study, become available at a reasonable price, they will help underdeveloped countries in many ways. In places that at present have no electricity, such reactors will supply power to develop small industries or to give light to towns. Near isolated mines, they will help extract ores from under the ground. In dry regions they will supply power to pump water for irrigation, and in marshy places they will help drain away the water. When these things come to pass, stretches of land that are now either deserts or marshes will produce food for undernourished populations.

3

Atomic power can be used to drive ships; for this purpose it has the advantage of being much more compact than any other fuel. Until the present time, stored fuels have always taken a great deal of space in large ships. In atomic ships, much of this space can be put to other uses, and the ship can make many trips without refueling.

The first two civilian boats propelled by atomic power have been built. In both, as in all future atomic boats, one or more reactors generate the heat needed to change water into steam, and the steam so produced drives the propellers.

The icebreaker *Lenin* of the Soviet Union has already gone to sea.

In July, 1959, at Camden, New Jersey, the merchant ship *Savannah* of the United States was launched in a typical ceremony by Mrs. Eisenhower, the President's wife. She smashed a white-clad bottle of champagne

Power from the atoms

on the stem of the ship, giving the signal for the workmen to trigger the releasing machinery. Swiftly the *Savannah* slid down into the Delaware River. It is able to sail almost fifteen times around the world without refueling. Its floating laboratory will study any difficulties that may arise and try to solve the problems of atomic propulsion. The results will be extremely useful in the building of future atomic-powered merchant fleets.

4

The heat produced when a reactor operates may be used directly to heat buildings. At the first conference on the peaceful uses of atomic energy, this use of reactors was among the topics discussed by scientists. A funny incident resulted. A woman who lived in Geneva read in the papers that atomic energy from uranium could be used to heat homes. She also read that the United States had set the price of natural uranium at forty dollars per kilogram, which is a little less than twenty dollars per pound. After a little figuring the woman came to the conclusion that uranium was quite an inexpensive fuel, and she went to the United States information desk at the conference to ask where she could buy uranium. The girls at the desk tried to explain that she could not "burn" uranium easily, in her furnace, like coal. They added that uranium "burns" only in reactors and that reactors are very expensive. The woman insisted, "You don't know how high my heating bill runs!" She did not realize that the cost of a reactor may run into tens of millions of dollars.

When reactors are eventually used to heat buildings, one reactor will serve a section of a city or a whole town.

14

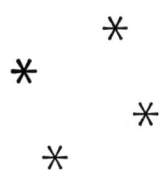

Radioisotopes for better living

1

When a reactor works and produces atomic energy, it also produces large amounts of radioactive substances. Many of these are today adding to man's knowledge, and giving him better health and better living conditions.

Ever since Henri Becquerel and Marie Curie discovered radioactivity at the end of the last century, radioactive substances have proved useful in many ways. For example, radium and other natural radioactive substances were used in luminous paints, especially paints for luminous watch dials. More important, scientists found that the strong radiations of radium could destroy the diseased cells of cancers and tumors, and soon doctors began to use small amounts of radium in the treatment of some forms of cancer.

In the early days of work in the field of radioactivity, natural radioactive substances were used as sources of bullets for atomic bombardment, and helped the physicists gain a deeper understanding of the atom. Radioactive substances were used also in other kinds of research. Their steady rate of decay, for instance, was a clock by which geologists could measure the age of rocks and of the earth itself.

As long as only natural radioactive substances—that is, those found in nature—were available, their use was limited by their scarcity and high cost. They are so scarce that Marie and Pierre Curie had to treat about seven tons of pitchblende in order to obtain a gram of a pure radium salt. Yet pitchblende is about 100,000 times richer in radioactive substances than the

Radioisotopes for better living

average material on the earth's crust. It is not surprising, then, that the price of radium has been as high as $135,000 per gram and that it was still $20,000 per gram in 1946. Other substances that could do the work of radium were even more expensive.

The first *artificial* radioactive substances were made in such extremely small amounts that scientists did not foresee any practical use for them. Slow neutrons multiplied by many times the amounts that could be made available, but many times almost nothing was still too little for practical purposes.

Shortly after the discovery of slow neutrons, Ernest Lawrence made much larger amounts of radioactive substances by using particles that were speeded up in his cyclotron. In 1935 he made an amount of radiosodium comparable to available amounts of natural radioactive substances. Radiosodium stirred up great interest for its possible uses in medicine. Doctors thought that it might be better than radium, for radium decays very slowly: its half life is about 1,600 years. Radium goes on giving off strong radiation for a long, long time, and for this reason, doctors cannot leave it inside a patient, but must remove it after a while. Otherwise, after destroying the diseased tissues, it would destroy the good ones, too. Radiosodium, on the other hand, has a half life of about twelve hours. Its activity stops altogether before it can do any harm.

When Lawrence announced he had made a sizable amount of radiosodium, a British authority, the physicist John Cockroft, commented that people should not expect too much of radiosodium. Lawrence's cyclotron was not yet producing it in sufficient quantities for widespread use in medicine. Besides, Cockroft said, its price was higher than that of radium itself, and would stay higher unless a cheaper way were found to induce radioactivity in sodium.

Only a few years later, Hahn and Strassmann discovered fission. And it was fission, which made reactors possible, that provided a much more economical way of inducing radioactivity. Reactors can produce not only radiosodium, but also a large number of other radioisotopes in great quantities and at a low cost.

Radioisotopes for better living

Reactors produce radioisotopes in two ways. First, while the reactors work, uranium atoms undergo fission, and divide into two almost equal parts. These two parts are not always the same. Fission may take place in at least thirty slightly different ways, each producing a different pair of radioactive atoms. At least sixty different radioisotopes form in uranium during fission.

Second, various substances may be placed inside a working reactor. The neutrons that are continuously freed by fission bombard these substances and make them become radioactive. In this way a reactor may produce a wide variety of radioisotopes in very large amounts.

Radioisotopes vary greatly in their properties. Each has a different half life, and some decay very fast, others very slowly. Some give off a very strong radiation, others a weak one. The radiation may travel far and penetrate thick layers of materials, or travel only a very short path. Some radioisotopes are poisonous and difficult to handle, others are safe and can be fed to plants, animals, and men. Biologists, doctors, and men in industry may choose the radioisotopes best suited to their purposes.

2

Radioisotopes are helping biologists to study how plants, animals, and men live, grow, and die; how they take up food and use it to build tissues; how they breathe; how the sap in plants and the blood in men move around to bring nourishment wherever needed; how cells and tissues become diseased and eventually die.

In many of their studies, biologists use radioisotopes as *tracers;* that is, substances which leave a track wherever they pass. As Hansel and Gretel marked their path in the woods with bread crumbs and pebbles, so tracer radioisotopes mark their path in living organisms with the radiation they give off. An example will make this clear.

Biologists are interested in finding out how fast

sodium travels in our bodies. Sodium is an element needed by most of our tissues and fluids. It is contained in ordinary salt which we add to food to get a large part of the sodium we need. Until recently biologists had no way of tracing the path of ordinary salt in our bodies, because the salt taken in on one day is identical with the salt taken in days before.

There is, however, a modern way of solving this problem. The biologist can expose some ordinary salt to bombardment of neutrons inside a reactor. Some atoms of sodium will become radioactive and change into radiosodium (sodium 24). And if we eat salt containing radiosodium, its path in our bodies will be marked by the radiation that radiosodium gives off. This radiation can make a Geiger counter click. Holding a Geiger counter outside our body, the biologist can follow the path of the sodium we have eaten.

In this case radiosodium is a kind of label attached to salt. So the salt containing radiosodium is called *labeled* salt. Using labeled salt, biologists have found that sodium travels at a very great speed in some of

The Story of Atomic Energy

our fluids; sodium injected into the blood stream of one arm takes only a few seconds to go through the heart and lungs and into the other arm. In seventy-five seconds it can be found in the sweat on our skin. A longer time is needed for sodium to get into our bones.

With other labeled substances as tracers, biologists have studied how the nutritive elements in our food are used by our bodies. They have learned that all tissues absorb fresh substances and discard old ones, and thus they are continuously being renewed. Before the use of radioisotopes, biologists believed that bones and teeth did not change; but they have now found that even bones and teeth are continuously being made over.

Labeled substances have helped the study of plants. Fertilizers labeled with radiophosphorus (phosphorus 32), for instance, have shown how the soil absorbs phosphorus, how much of it the plants can take up from the soil, what part of the phosphorus that plants take up comes from the fertilizer and what part from

Radioisotopes for better living

the phosphorus that was already in the soil. In other studies with radioisotopes, biologists have proved that plants take their nourishment not only through the roots, but also through the foliage, fruit, twigs, trunk, and flowers.

In a similar way biologists have studied how animals make use of the food they eat. Often these studies have helped in the planning of a diet for cattle and poultry that has improved the quality or the quantity of meat, milk, and eggs. The cow has been the object of special attention because of the great importance of her milk. With radioisotopes, biologists have followed the journey of food elements in the cow's body, observed how food is digested, and which products of digestion reach the udder to form milk. Once they knew what substances were going into the milk, they were able to produce it in an artificial cow: an artificial heart and lung pumped these substances into an udder that made the milk.

Scientists have said that radioisotopes are the most important new tool of research they have had since the microscope. Through the miscroscope they can see still pictures: single cells, for instance, and cells fastened together in tissues. With radioisotopes, scientists see moving pictures; they can follow all the steps by which a living organism forms these cells and tissues from the simple substances in its food.

3

Sometimes biologists cannot label an organic compound, either because exposure to radiation would damage it, or for other reasons. One such compound is cholesterol, which is found in animals' and men's bodies. It may be one of the causes of cancer and hardening of the arteries.

Biologists could not make radioactive cholesterol in the laboratory or in a reactor, but they found another way to label it. Radiocarbon was fed to certain bacteria that made a substance called acetic acid. The bacteria that were fed on radiocarbon made radioactive acetic acid. The biologists then fed the radioactive acetic acid to pigs, which produced radioactive cholesterol in their blood. The radioactive cholesterol was extracted from the pigs' blood and used in research.

Plants likewise can produce labeled compounds. Plants absorb carbon from the carbon dioxide in the air. Then, with the help of sunlight, they combine carbon dioxide with water and food substances to form a large number of organic products containing carbon. Scientists have built little greenhouses in which the carbon dioxide in the air contains some radiocarbon (carbon 14).

Plants grown in these greenhouses have yielded labeled products: sugar beets have produced labeled sugar; tobacco plants have produced labeled nicotine. Other plants have yielded radioactive morphine, vitamin C, and other compounds that are used to prepare labeled drugs. Labeled drugs have helped scientists to understand how each drug acts in our body.

Radiocarbon is especially suited for labeling drugs. Plants and animals may take a long time to produce

The Story of Atomic Energy

the labeled materials that go into these drugs. If radioisotopes other than radiocarbon have been used, they may decay entirely and lose their radioactivity when the drugs are stored for long periods. Radiocarbon, instead, decays slowly. Its half life is 5,600 years. In the time that passes from the moment plants or animals take it up to the moment the labeled drug is used, its radioactivity does not decrease very much. Its radiation is weak and does not harm plants, animals, or men, and this is another reason why radiocarbon is a good label.

Carbon 14—radiocarbon—is not only made in reactors; it is also found in nature. Willard Libby and a group of scientists working with him discovered it in the sewers of Baltimore some years ago.

A few years later, the study of radiocarbon led Libby to find a method for telling the age of mummies, old bones, fossils, and other things that had once been alive. Libby explained this method, which he called *carbon dating*, in a lecture at the first International Conference on the Peaceful Uses of Atomic

Radioisotopes for better living

Energy in Geneva. He startled his audience when he unwrapped an assortment of petrified-looking objects, among which was a shoe "woven of grass rope by an ancient artisan, some 9,000 years ago in . . . the State of Oregon." The shoe was one of three hundred pairs of shoes found in a cave that had been buried by an ancient volcano. Libby also had a piece of frayed rope from Peru, two thousand years old; and the droppings, ten thousand years old, of some extinct prehistoric animal of Nevada. He had determined the age of these things by carbon dating.

He explained that radiocarbon is always being formed in the highest part of the atmosphere when neutrons in the cosmic rays strike the nitrogen in the air. The carbon dioxide in our atmosphere always contains a small amount of radiocarbon, which is taken up by plants, and by animals and men that feed on plants. All living organisms contain the same proportion of radiocarbon. When they die, they stop taking up radiocarbon, and this begins to decay and disappear. The proportion of radiocarbon decreases. A

The Story of Atomic Energy

mummy that has been dead 5,600 years contains half the carbon 14 that it contained when it was a living person. From the content of radiocarbon in old objects, Libby could tell how long ago they had been living matter.

4

Radioisotopes are becoming more and more important in the diagnosis and treatment of disease. In the treatment of many forms of cancer, doctors place a small amount of a radioactive substance inside the cancer tissue, or near it. The radiation given off by this substance destroys the cancer tissues. In the past, radium was the substance for cancer treatment, but now doctors may choose from a large variety of radioisotopes. Radiogold, radiophosphorus, radioiridium, and radiocobalt are among those most frequently used for this purpose.

Like biologists, doctors often use radioisotopes as

tracers. Among the tracer isotopes useful to medicine is radiosodium, with which salt can be labeled. One use of labeled salt is to determine whether a patient's blood is flowing normally in his blood vessels, or whether it is being slowed down at some point.

To get this information, doctors inject a patient's arm with labeled salt, thus forcing it into the blood stream. Then they place a Geiger counter near one of the patient's feet. If the blood flows freely, as it should, the counter will soon begin to click faster and faster, showing that more and more radiosodium is reaching the foot. But if a blood vessel is narrowed or clogged at some point, the counter will indicate that the radiosodium is reaching the foot more slowly than it should. The doctors will then know that the blood has met an obstacle, and by moving the counter to different parts of the patient's body they will be able to locate the obstacle.

Sodium, we have seen, is taken up by most of our tissues and fluids. Other elements are not as evenly distributed, but gather mainly in one part or tissue of the body. Thus, for instance, most of the iodine in our body is taken up by the thyroid, a gland at the front of the neck that plays an important role in our health. If it does not work well, it may cause goiter, idiocy, or heart disease.

If a doctor wishes to know whether a patient's thyroid is functioning properly, he gives his patient a drink containing a little radioiodine (iodine 131) and then places a Geiger counter over the patient's neck. By measuring the radioactivity in the thyroid, he is able to tell whether the gland is taking up the normal amount of iodine, or whether it is taking up too much or too little of it.

With a very sensitive counter, the doctor may even make a "map" of the thyroid, showing which parts work well and which do not. If he should find that the thyroid is overworking or is cancerous, he may give the patient a stronger dose of radioiodine. The radiation from the radioiodine will destroy some of the diseased tissue of the thyroid.

Radioiodine is used also to locate brain tumors, one

Radioisotopes for better living

of the most serious and painful forms of cancer. In this case radioiodine is not given by mouth, but is injected into the blood stream. Because a tumor has a greater blood supply than the normal brain tissues, more radioiodine will gather in the tumor than in the rest of the brain. Several counters placed around the head of the patient will reveal the spot from which the most intense radiation comes. Surgeons often locate brain tumors by this method before operating.

In one treatment of brain tumors doctors do not use an existing radioisotope, but *make one* right inside the tumor. To do this, they give the patient an injection of boron; tumor tissues take up boron much faster than normal tissues, and for a while there is much more boron in the tumor than in the rest of the brain. Some ten minutes after he has had the shot of boron, the patient is made to lie on a reactor, with his head carefully placed over a small hole in the shielding. Out of this hole comes a strong beam of neutrons that bombard the boron in the tumor. Boron atoms hit by neutrons give off alpha particles, which destroy the tumor cells. The path of the alpha particles is very short, and they stop before they can reach and harm other tissues. A special medical reactor was built at the Brookhaven National Laboratory for this treatment of brain tumors.

Doctors have long used x-rays both for taking x-ray pictures and for treating diseases, but today radioisotopes, such as radiocobalt, are often used instead of x-rays. Many hospitals, both in the United States and in other countries, are equipped with cobalt units. These contain large amounts of radiocobalt—cobalt 60—that is made in reactors. Radiocobalt gives off very strong gamma rays, which are similar to x-rays. Cobalt units can do the work of very powerful x-ray machines, and they are easier to handle and much less expensive. The rays from cobalt units can be directed with greater precision to the part of the patient's body that needs treatment.

5

We have seen only a few examples, out of a very large number, of the ways in which biologists and doctors use radioisotopes. Biology and medicine are only two of the many fields in which radioisotopes are useful. To United States industry they are bringing very substantial savings—$500,000 a year, according to an estimate made by the Atomic Energy Commission in 1957. (The benefits in biology and medicine cannot be measured in terms of dollars.) In agriculture the use of irradiated seeds, the experiments to produce better crops and livestock, and the progress being made in doing away with the pests that afflict plants and animals, are already producing great financial returns. In physics, chemistry, metallurgy, and in other branches of science, radioisotopes are enlarging and deepening the understanding of matter and of its behavior.

A full list of the present uses of radioisotopes would be very long indeed. As more reactors are built all over

The Story of Atomic Energy

the world, they will yield greater and greater amounts of radioisotopes. These, in turn, will become less expensive and available to larger sections of the world. Only man's imagination will limit their uses and the benefits they will bring to mankind.

The picture of the future is very bright. Yet we must add a few words of caution. Radioactivity is dangerous. It may cause skin burns and it may destroy good tissues, as it destroys diseased ones. It may cause illness that could be passed on to our children and grandchildren. In cases of severe exposure it may even cause death.

In the early days of radioactivity, scientists were not aware of these dangers. Marie and Pierre Curie, after having worked for a while with radioactive materials, noticed that their fingers were reddened and swollen and that the skin was peeling off. Henri Becquerel carried a small tube with radium in his vest pocket, and was surprised to find a burn on his chest. Other early workers also reported burns and injuries of various kinds.

Radioisotopes for better living

The strange fact about radiation is that it can harm without causing pain, which is the warning signal we expect from injuries. Pain makes us pull back our hands from a flame or from a very hot object, but a person handling radioactive materials has no way of telling whether he is touching something too "hot" for safety. Besides, the "burns" or other injuries that radioactivity produces may not appear for weeks. A person may have been injured and not know it for some time.

Today scientists are fully aware of these dangers. They are steadily finding new means of protecting themselves and others from radioactivity. It may well be that in the race between production of radioactivity and production of means of protection, the second will be the winner.

Our modern atomic laboratories are built for safety. Their walls are very thick. The rooms in which radioactivity is handled are separated from others by heavy lead doors. Large signs reading "Danger—Radiation" indicate the unsafe parts of buildings. Counters and other

The Story of Atomic Energy

instruments continuously measure the radiation and give off signals when it becomes too strong. Each worker wears a special badge that shows the amount of radiation to which he has been exposed.

In the rooms in which radioisotopes are separated and handled, workers may wear plastic outfits that look like divers' suits. They may handle material under water with long tongs; water, we know, stops the radiation and protects the workers.

In some cases, a worker may not be in the same room with the dangerous material he is working on. Instead, he stands outside the room and uses "magic hands." These are instruments that transmit the motions of his hands to pincers or similar tools on the other side of a wall. Through a window in the wall he can see what he is doing. The window glass may be three feet thick. With his magic hands the worker can make a delicate analysis, separate radioactive substances from one another, fill bottles with them, and screw caps on the bottles.

Radioisotopes for better living

All radioisotopes are prepared in this way, or by other methods of remote control. They are then placed inside heavy lead containers through which radiation cannot pass, and shipped to wherever they are to be used.

6

This is the end of our story. The atomic age is still at its dawning. Fewer than twenty years have passed since its birth on that day in December 1942 when man for the first time released atomic energy in a chain reaction—enough atomic energy to light at most a small flashlight bulb. Twenty years are only a flash of time in comparison with the age of mankind, which is measured in millions of years. And yet in this flash of time, atomic energy has accomplished a great deal. It helped the United States and its allies to win the Second World War.

The Story of Atomic Energy

It is now offering to mankind—the whole of mankind—more power, better health, more food, more knowledge. It has furthered scientific and technological collaboration between all countries of the world.

The atomic age, young as it is, is well under way.

Index

Accelerators, 64
Acetic acid, radioactive, 165
Advisory Committee on Uranium, 72–73
Alpha particles, atoms bombarded by, 26–27, 30–32, 35
  brain tumor cells destroyed by, 171–72
  discovery of, 20
  energy of, 23
  heaviness of, 20
  positive charges of, 20
  role in decay of elements, 21–22
Alpha rays, 20–21
Aluminum, bombarded by alpha particles, 32
  radioactive, 39

Anderson, Herbert, 77, 82, 124
Arsenic, radioactive, 39
Atom(s), bombarded by alpha particles, 26–27, 30–32
  structure of, 27–28
Atomic bomb, 91–92, 98, 130
Atomic energy, amount in radioactivity, 23–24
  fission as key to, 54, 61–62
  for heating buildings, 153–54
  peaceful uses of, 132–54
  power generated from, 142–44
  as revolutionary concept, 21, 23
  ships driven by, 152–53
Atomic Energy Commission, 173
Atomic mass, 28–29
  of barium, 52

Index

Atomic mass (*continued*)
  of helium, 29
  of hydrogen, 29
  of uranium, 29, 51
Atomic number, 28
  of barium, 51–53
  of helium, 29
  of hydrogen, 29
  of krypton, 53
  of radium, 52
  of uranium, 29, 51–52
Atomic pile, 75–78, 81–82, 99
  built inside balloon, 83–84
  cadmium rod in, 85–86, 112
  coolant for, 112–13
  graphite for, 75–78, 82–83
  at Hanford, 111–15
  shielding of, 112, 115
  successful Chicago experiment with, 84–91
  uranium in, 75, 78, 82
Atomic power plant, 144–45
  English, 147–48
  Soviet, 146–47
  United States, 149–50
Atomic ship, 152–53
Atomic theory, Dalton's, 6, 8–9
Atomos, 5
Atoms-for-Peace Plan, 134–37

Barium, atomic number of, 51–53
  as product of uranium bombardment, 51–53
Becquerel, Henri, 10–12, 14, 18, 32, 155, 174
Berkeley cyclotron, 96–97
Beryllium, bombarded by alpha particles, 26–27, 30–31, 35–36
Beta particles, 20–21, 23, 41, 97–98
Beta rays, 20–21
Bohr, Niels, 27–28, 55–59, 84

  at Geneva Conference on Atomic Energy, 139
  at Los Alamos, 125–27
Boiling water reactor, 150
Boron, in treatment of brain tumor, 171–72
Boyle, Robert, 6
Brain tumor, and radioisotopes, 171–72
British Mission, at Los Alamos, 127–28
Brookhaven National Laboratory, 172

Cadmium rod, 85–86, 112
Calder Hill reactor, 147
California, University of, 65, 96, 98
Cancer, treatment of, with radium, 17, 156, 168
  with variety of radioisotopes, 168
Carbon, as chemical element, 7
Carbon dating, 166–68
Chadwick, James, 27, 30, 127
Chain reaction, nuclear, 63, 66–67, 70, 72, 74–75, 78–79
  first, 87–89
Chicago, University of, 80–81
Chlorine, as chemical element, 7
  radioactive phosphorus obtained from, 39
Cholesterol, radioactive, 164–65
Clinton Engineering Works, 103–05
Cobalt, radioactive, 168, 172
Cockroft, John, 158
Cold war, 133
Columbia River, 108, 112–13, 115
Columbia University, 58, 64–67, 73, 75, 77–78, 81, 99
Compounds, chemical, 7–9

* 180 *

Index

Compton, Arthur H., 79–80, 88–89
Conant, James, 88–89
Cosmic rays, 167
Curie, Eve, 13, 33
Curie, Marie, 13–17, 19, 31–33, 155–56, 174
Curie, Pierre, 13–16, 19, 156, 174
Cyclotron, 64–65, 140
  Berkeley, 96
  giant, 105

Dalton, John, 6–9, 21
Decay, defined, 22
Democritus, 4–6, 21
Dresden (Illinois) reactor, 149–50
Drugs, labeled, 165–66

Einstein, Albert, 55–56, 69
  letter to Roosevelt, 70–71, 88
Eisenhower, Dwight D., 134–35, 149
Electrons, as beta particles, 20
  discovery of, 18
  motion around nucleus, 27–28
Element(s), 7–8
  changes in, after bombardment of atoms, 21–23, 30–31
  isotopes of, 29–30
  No. *93*, 40, 45, 48, 59–60, 95, 97–98
  No. *94*, 48, 98
  radioactive, 11–17, 20–23
  total number of, 8
  transuranic, 48–49, 51

Farrell, General, quoted, 129–30
Fermi, Enrico, 34, 36–38, 40, 42–46, 58–59, 64–65, 67–68, 73–77, 83, 91–92, 96
  atomic pile experiment directed by, 85–89
  at Los Alamos, 124–25, 127

Fission of uranium, 53–56
  and chain reaction, 63, 66–67, 70, 72, 74–75, 78–79
  Einstein's interest in, 70
  energy freed by, 58–59
  German research on, 66–67, 69, 71, 79
  as key to atomic energy, 54, 61–62
  neutrons produced by, 61–62
  secrecy of U.S. research on, 72, 80–81, 92, 100–02, 118–28
  See also Uranium; Uranium *235*
Fissionable materials, 93, 98, 134
  as nuclear fuels, 144
  U.S. shipment to foreign countries, 137–38
Fluorine, radioactive, 38
Frisch, Otto, 54–56, 58, 127
Fuel elements, in reactor, 146–47

Galileo, 6
Gamma rays, 20–22, 24, 172
Gaseous diffusion, 103–04
Geiger counter, 37
Geneva Conference on Peaceful Uses of Atomic Energy, 138–41, 166–67
Goodyear Rubber Company, 82
Graphite, for atomic pile, 75–78, 82–83
Groves, Leslie R., 91–92, 100, 108, 112, 118–19, 123–24

Hahn, Otto, 46–55, 97, 140, 158
Half life, defined, 23
Hanford, 109–17, 128, 130
Hanford Engineering Works, 110, 115–16
Helium, atom of, 29
Hiroshima, 130
Hitler, Adolf, 49–50, 56–58, 67, 72

* 181 *

Index

Hydrogen, atom of, 19–20, 28–29, 42
 as chemical element, 7
 nucleus of, 42–43, 64
 unsatisfactory for chain reaction, 75

International Conference on Peaceful Uses of Atomic Energy, 138–41, 166–67
Iodine, radioactive, 39, 170
Iron, as chemical element, 8
 radioactive manganese obtained from, 39–40
Iron Curtain, 133, 138
Isotopes, defined, 29
 difficulty of separating, 94–95
 radioactive, see Radioisotopes

Japan, surrender of, 130
Joliot, Frederic, 31–33
Joliot-Curie, Irene, 13–14, 31–33, 48–50

Krypton, atomic number of, 53

Labeled substances, 161–66, 169
Lawrence, Ernest O., 64, 96, 105–06, 140, 157–58
Lenin (atomic icebreaker), 152
Libby, Willard, 166–68
Los Alamos, 118–28, 130

"Magic hands," 176
Magnet, for separating uranium 235, 104–07
Manganese, radioactive, 39–40
Manhattan District, 91, 102, 115, 120
Mass, of atom, 28
Medical reactor, 172
Meitner, Lise, 46–50, 53–56, 58, 97, 127

Metallurgical Laboratory, 80–82, 88
Molecule, formation of, 9
Mussolini, Benito, 58

Nagasaki, 130
Neptunium, 98–99
Neutrons, in atomic pile, 77
 boron bombarded by, in treatment of tumor, 171–72
 captured by cadmium, 85–86
 discovery of, 27, 30–31
 mass of, 28
 nuclei bombarded by, 34–38, 41–42, 45, 47–48, 51–53, 74
 in nucleus, 28
 production of, 35–36, 61–62, 65–66
 slow, 42, 44, 74–76, 97, 157
Nitrogen, bombarded by alpha particles, 26, 30
Nuclear fuels, 144, 146
Nucleus of atom, 27–28

Oak Ridge, 102, 104, 106, 128, 130
Oppenheimer, J. Robert, 120, 127
 as director of Los Alamos project, 124
Oxygen, as chemical element, 7

"Package" reactor, 151
Paraffin, 42
Pearl Harbor, 79
Phosphorescence, 10
Phosphorus, glow of, 10
 radioactive, 32, 39, 162, 168
Pile, atomic, *see* Atomic pile
Pitchblende, radioactive elements in, 14–16, 19, 156–57
Plutonium, 98–100, 109
 half life of, 98
 separated from uranium, 114–15

* 182 *

Index

Polonium, 15, 17
Princeton University, 58–59, 69
Protoactinium, 46–47
Protons, discovery of, 26, 30
   mass of, 28
   in nucleus, 28
   used in cyclotron, 65

Radioactivity, artificial, 32–34, 157
   Curies' research on, 14–17, 31
   dangers of, 113–14, 174–76
   decay through, 21–23
   discovery of, 11–14
   Joliots' research on, 31–33
   Rutherford's research on, 18–23, 25–26, 30
Radiocarbon, 164–68
Radiocobalt, 168, 172
Radioiodine, 39, 170
Radioiridium, 168
Radioisotopes, 32, 38–39, 97, 135–36
   in agriculture, 173
   for better living, 155–65, 168–74
   biology studied with aid of, 160–65
   in industry, 173
   in medicine, 168–72
   obtained from reactors, 158–59
   remote control of, 176–77
   as tracers, 160–64, 169–71
   varying properties of, 159–60
Radiophosphorus, 32, 39, 162, 168
Radiosodium, 157–58, 161–62, 169
Radium, atomic number of, 52
   in cancer treatment, 17, 156, 168
   discovery of, 15
   as "gun" for bombarding atoms, 26
   half life of, 23, 157
   in pitchblende, 15–16, 19
   price of, 36, 157
   and radon, 22
   uses of, 17
Radon, 22
   half life of, 37
   in neutron "gun," 37
Reactor(s), 136, 144–49
   boiling water, 150
   cost of, 154
   medical, 172
   "package," 151
   radioisotopes produced by, 158–59
Richland, 109–10
Roosevelt, Franklin D., 70–71, 79, 88, 130
Rutherford, Ernest, 18–23, 25–28, 30, 47, 55, 62

Salt, as chemical compound, 7
   labeled, 161, 169
   See also Sodium
Savannah (atomic ship), 152–53
Second World War, outbreak of, 71
   U.S. participation in, 79
   use of atomic bomb in, 130
Segré, Emilio, 37, 96, 124, 126–27
Shippingport reactor, 149
Silicon, radioactive aluminum obtained from, 39
Silver, bombarded by neutrons, 41–44
   for Oak Ridge magnet, 106–07
Smyth, H. D., 123
Sodium, as chemical element, 7
   needed by body fluids and tissues, 161, 169–70
   radioactive, 39, 157–58, 161–62, 169
   See also Salt
Strassmann, Fritz, 48–55, 97, 158
Sugar, as chemical compound, 7
Szilard, Leo, 68–76, 88, 92

* 183 *

Index

Thomson, J. J., 18–19
Thorium, radioactivity of, 14
Thyroid gland, and radioiodine, 170
Tracer radioisotopes, 160–64, 169–71
Transuranic elements, 48–49, 51
Trinity explosion, 128–30
Truman, Harry S., 130, 134

United Nations, 138
  and Eisenhower's Atoms-for-Peace Plan, 134–35, 137
Uranium, atom of, 29
  atomic mass of, 29, 51
  atomic number of, 29, 51–52
  in atomic pile, 75, 78, 82
  bombarded by neutrons, 39–40, 45–48, 51–53, 96–97
  Fermi's warning on explosion of, 68
  fissionable, 93
  half life of, 23
  isotopes of, 30, 39, 93–98
  price of, 153–54
  radioactivity of, 11–12, 17–19
  See also Fission of uranium
Uranium *235*, 93–95, 97, 100
  separated from uranium *238*, 94–95, 103–06
Uranium *238*, 93–94, 96–97, 103, 114
Uranium *239*, 97
  half life of, 97

Veksler, Vladimir, 140

Water, as chemical compound, 7, 9
  as coolant, 112–13
  radioactivity of silver increased by, 44
Weil, George, 85–87, 112
Wigner, Eugene, 68–71, 88
Wood, Leona, 85

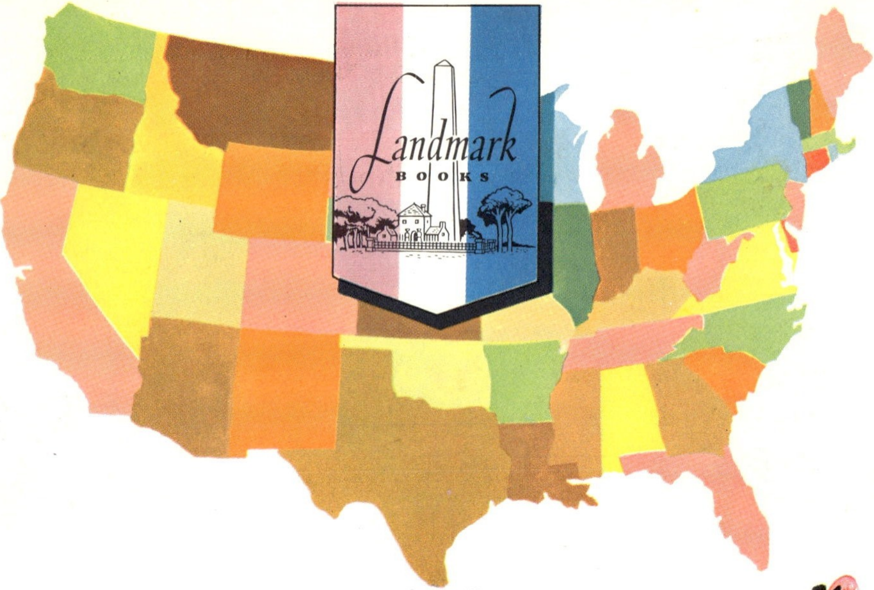
Landmark
BOOKS

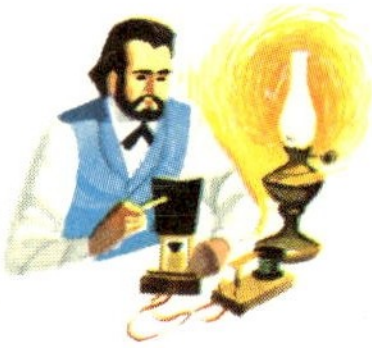

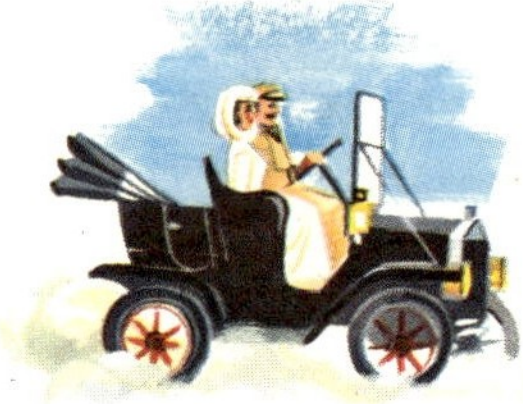

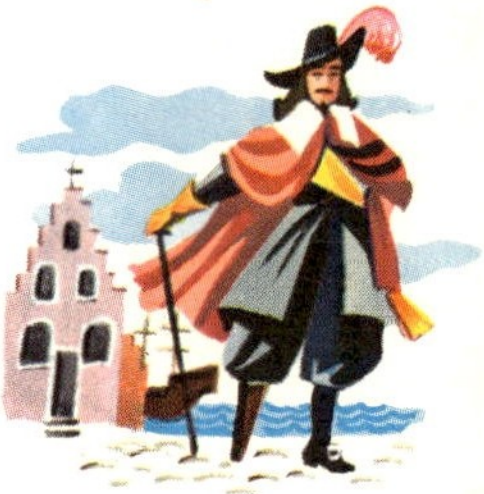

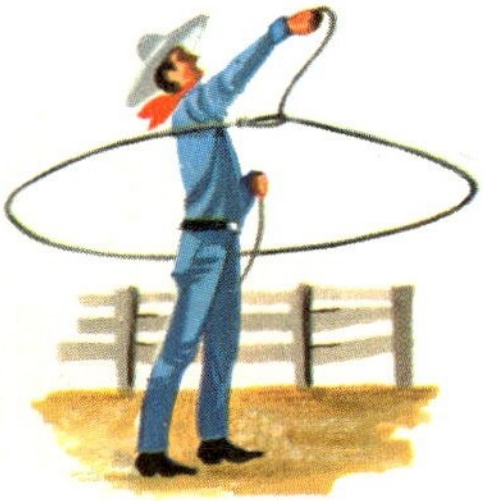

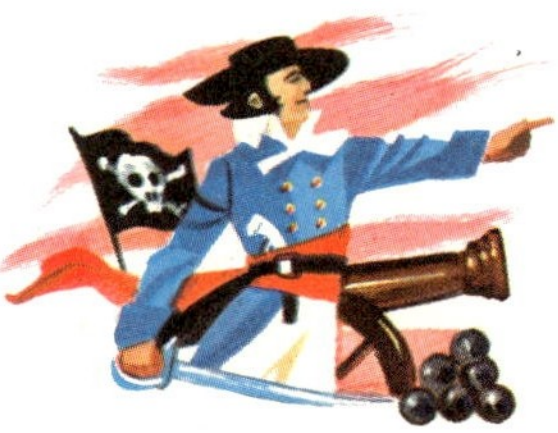

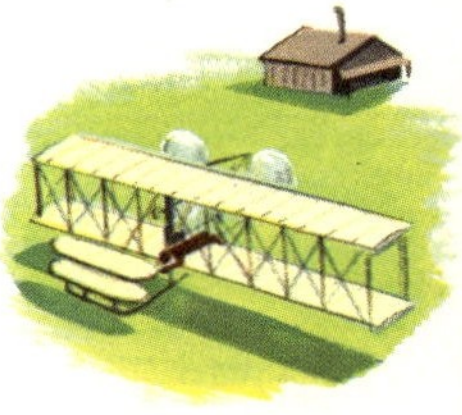

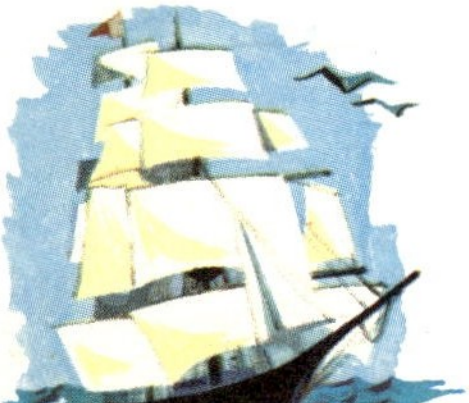

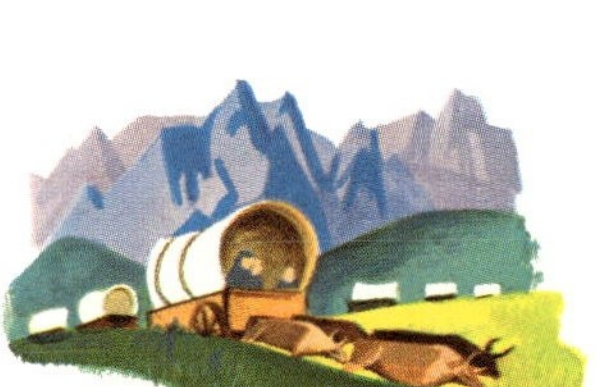

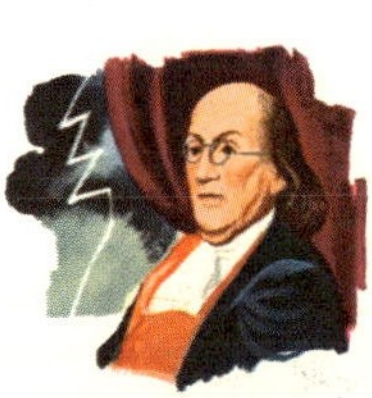